JANE ADDAMS
Pioneer for Social Justice
by
CORNELIA MEIGS
author of INVINCIBLE LOUISA

This is a biography of a woman of action —a woman who inspired others and worked with them to make city and country, the nation and the world better places in which to live. It tells about people who *did* things to correct bad social conditions in the early twentieth century and late nineteenth, and what they did. Thus it is much more than a chronology of birth, life, and death. It is the record of an era.

In his biography of his aunt, Jane Addams, soon after her death, James Weber Linn said, "It is to be hoped that some day some scholar, completely acquainted with the history . . . of American civilization in the last half century, will offer a picture of it as illuminated by her life, for I think she threw more light into its dark places than anyone else."

Cornelia Meigs has used that light in this book for, as she says, "It is time to look once more at the height and depth of the good she did for her own time and ours."

tion, chosen as an *outstanding book for older readers (B Group).*

Books by Cornelia Meigs

THE TRADE WIND

SWIFT RIVERS

INVINCIBLE LOUISA

THE GREAT DESIGN

JANE ADDAMS

JANE ADDAMS

Pioneer for Social Justice

FROM A DRAWING IN THE WASHINGTON *Daily News*

JANE ADDAMS

Pioneer for Social Justice

A Biography by
Cornelia Meigs

Little, Brown and Company—Boston—Toronto

Published simultaneously in Canada
by Little, Brown & Company (Canada) Limited

PRINTED IN THE UNITED STATES OF AMERICA

To
Lily Ross Taylor
An Eminent and Inspiring Scholar,
An Incomparable Friend

To Mercy, Pity, Peace and Love
All pray in their distress;
And to these virtues of delight
Return their thankfulness.

William Blake

Contents

JANE ADDAMS

Pioneer for Social Justice

I

Open Skies

The work to which Jane Addams gave her whole life was so
great a task that she herself knew well it would need more
than one generation to complete it. In spite of a lapse of
years, she really belongs to our own time. It is in the
present day that so much of what she and her associates
began has come to the fullness of those results which she so
confidently foresaw. It has remained for another generation
and part of one more to reap the hundredfold harvest of
the seed she and her fellow workers planted and faithfully
watered. Some of her efforts were devoted to what she
conceived on her own initiative, some were brought about
by able and often indispensable support of the work of
others. In one field, however, there was no one before her.
This was in her challenging belief in the rights and needs
of young people.

She was firm in her conviction that one of the greatest
things wrong with the society of her day — and there was
much indeed that needed desperately to be put right —
was the neglect and misunderstanding of what youth

needed in its difficult and troubled progress to maturity. She had helpers as she worked to remedy this lack, but she also had many hands against her.

Various accounts of her life were published in the period shortly after her death. To these we may add her own "Autobiographical Notes" contained in the first part of her book *Twenty Years at Hull House*. But what her life accomplished can only be measured today in the coming to fruition of what she set out to do for the society which needed her so greatly. It is time to look once more at the height and depth of the good she did for her own time and ours. To do so is to pay her a large debt, long and justly owed.

The happy childhood of Jane Addams had direct bearing on the kind and quality of her later life, even though the two seem poles apart. She was brought up in a small country town, possibly the best of all kinds of places in which an impressionable little girl could spend her early years. She was supremely happy there, while she was learning many things that she would make use of later. Being herself and no one else, she decided early and firmly what she wanted to do with her future, although she was long puzzled about how she was to set about it.

In the end, by definite choice she would spend all the years of her very active working life in a city slum, with tumbledown tenements about her, the noise of heavy carts rumbling over ill-paved streets, and a babel of voices chattering in a dozen or more foreign tongues coming in at the open windows. She loved it all; she found it exciting. She could not have done what she did for her fellow men had it not been for her freedom of spirit in those early days, and for the wise guidance of her father. An imaginative little girl, with a congenial playmate close to her own age and a wide green countryside for her playground, can store up very bright memories, especially with just such a father to watch over her growing up. As she looked back in later years she found indeed much to remember.

One of her two earliest and most vivid recollections was a mere flash of memory, never forgotten. It was of a morning before she was three years old when she came abruptly into her father's study and found him deep in low-voiced talk with a colored man. Negroes were not very plentiful in northern Illinois at that time, although its southern boundary touched the slave-holding state of Kentucky. Her father motioned to her that they were not to be disturbed and she slipped out again. Later when he opened the door to her, the visitor was gone. He called her in and told her that she was to speak to no one, absolutely no one, of the dark stranger who had been there. She gave him her word and kept it until after her father was dead and she was grown up.

Perhaps nobody ever told her in plain words the exact meaning of what she had seen. But later she realized that her father was one of those who helped carry on the "Underground Railroad," that chain of refuges reaching from the states that bordered the slavery region all the way up to Canada. Runaway slaves were smuggled from town to town until they passed beyond the boundary of the United States and reached a country where they were free from capture. Dire punishment awaited runaways if they were caught. There were also heavy penalties for those who helped them to get away, fines and possible imprisonment. A bounty was offered to any person who would give information against someone who could be proved to be "running slaves" and assisting these pitiful fugitives to their freedom. It took courage to give such help and a certain adroitness to keep from being found out. Yet John Addams, prosperous mill-owner in a little town where most people knew all about their neighbors' activities, and in spite of the racketeers who made money out of informing, was never betrayed by proven evidence.

When he was twenty-two years old and newly married, John Huy Addams had brought his young wife out to Illinois from Kreidersville, Pennsylvania, in the summer of 1844. In his boyhood he had been apprenticed to a miller and had thoroughly learned the business of owning and operating both saw- and gristmills, the latter being called in those days "flouring mills." There was a general drifting westward of adventurous spirits in the eighteen-forties and -fifties. Young men were looking for larger opportunities than existed in the smaller towns of the East.

The two Addamses traveling by Great Lakes steamer, arrived in Chicago in August of 1844. They gave but brief inspection to the town rising at the lower end of Lake Michigan, only just chartered as a city. It was a tumultuous place, bursting with energy and industrial enterprise, where sudden fortunes were being made, and on occasion, as suddenly lost.

Feeling no temptation to remain and settle there, John Addams bought a horse and buggy and set out with his bride for Freeport, in one of the northern counties of Illinois. Here he had cousins at whose place he could make headquarters while he searched for the right spot in which to set up business. He found it difficult to choose, for he had only a very small capital to invest. He put down in his diary, "I hope and pray God some permanent light may soon appear." For the two of them he wished to "settle down in life to do honor to God and selves." It was nearly Christmas when, after weeks of exploring various places and possibilities, he bought a sawmill and a gristmill and eighty acres of land on the Cedar River not far from Freeport. He had brought a bag of Norway pine seeds from home and planted them at once on a hill by the creek — his hill now — as his first act of ownership. There was no town there at that time; Freeport was six miles away.

The midwestern landscape can be very beautiful where along the watercourses the rolling prairies rise into broken hills crowned with woods. Cedar Creek, for it was only by courtesy a river, flows into the Rock River, so-called because it is rare for a western stream to have so stony a bed. It, in turn, runs down to the great Mississipi. Towns were few in that stretch of country, although Rockford, twenty miles from the Addams mills, was of considerable size. With the growing prosperity of John Addams and his mills, a town soon sprang up called Cedarville. John Addams was a man of real ability, and under his hand business went well at once.

His family name had formerly been spelled Adams. It belonged to an Adams who came from Oxfordshire in England to settle in Pennsylvania on a grant of land received from William Penn. He was John Adams's great-grandfather. His son Isaac added the extra "d" to the name, to keep from being confused with a cousin who was also called Isaac. Isaac's grandson John Addams, spelled with two "d's," became very promptly the leading man of his small neighborhood. He built himself a large, comfortable brick house on the hillside above Cedar Creek. Here his four daughters came into the world, the youngest being Jane.

She was born September 6, 1860, entering a stormy world in which the question of slavery and the bitter arguments for and against it, lay like a blight over the whole country. A desperate war loomed ever closer. When she was little more than two years old, Jane lost her mother and so had no real recollection of her.

Sarah Addams had grown to be one of the essential figures in Cedarville's little community. She has been spoken of as having "a heart ever alive to the wants of the poor." She had gone to the help of a sick neighbor when she was too close to the expected arrival of a baby of her own, and died a week later along with her newborn child.

The household was ably taken over by the eldest sister Mary, who was only seventeen, yet gave unstinted affection and attention to the care of little Jennie. There was between these two the closest bond of understanding and love, which comforted and supported Jane even after she was grown and famous. The other daughters were Alice and Martha, called the beauty of the family, who died at the age of sixteen while she was at Rockford Seminary.

Jane's second vivid recollection of her early childhood was of the morning of April 1865 when she came into her father's study to find him openly weeping. It was the first time she realized that grown-up people could and did shed tears. He told her at once that President Lincoln was dead, shot at Ford's Theatre in Washington the night before. People of the present generation know clearly enough what the assassination of a President can mean, the stark unbelief of the first minutes, then the trooping in of sorrow and questioning. Who did it, why, what will happen now? Four

Presidents have been assassinated, but Lincoln was the first.

The shocking news which reached little Cedarville was accompanied immediately by descriptions of the wild panic which swept over Washington in that tragic night, as terror flew on the wings of frantic rumor. There was a plot, so the word ran, to murder the whole of the Cabinet, to seize the government and so turn back the victory which had been so happily celebrated only a few days before.

The stories grew — Secretary of State Seward had actually been attacked and wounded; news spread quickly that he was dead; so, it was vaguely reported, were many others. The wild tales reached fantastic proportions and only at last died down into brokenhearted mourning as Lincoln's funeral cortège moved slowly across the country to bring him home to Springfield.

Jane's father, although no real politician, was elected over and over again without opposition to the Illinois legislature. He sat in it at Springfield through those stormy years that preceded the outbreak of the Civil War and during the whole of that unhappy conflict. It was thus that he came to know and revere Abraham Lincoln. John Addams had recognized early the great gifts dwelling in this tall, awkward, quiet man and he had been a part of the convention for organizing the new Republican Party that was to make Abraham Lincoln President.

Later her father showed Jane a slim packet of letters, long treasured and all signed *A. Lincoln.* They invariably began, "My dear Mr. double-d-ed Addams." Lincoln wrote to Mr. Addams occasionally to ask about the political situation in that northern county and what the temper of the people was.

Her father's grief and his frequent talks with her later concerning this greatly beloved friend and President made little Jane take him as one of her heroes. As she grew older, she partook more and more of her father's understanding of this great sad man. She came to share with him Lincoln's sense of people, of people as persons and individuals, of people of all classes and kinds, particularly the simplest and poorest ones, and of people as a whole making up a great nation.

Jane has said that she always thought of herself as an ugly child, although there is no real evidence that she actually was. It was true that her hair did not curl when curls, long ones, even if created by means of water and a curling stick, were the vogue for children of her time. She was small for her age and very slim. She suffered — very literally suffered — from a slight curvature of the spine, which was scarcely noticeable but entailed holding her head a little on one side. It was said to have been due to abscesses of the spine. She was convinced that this constituted ugliness and she developed the odd idea that strangers meeting her tall good-looking father would be amazed to see that he had such an ill-favored child.

So fully did she love him that she sought to spare him any necessity of being ashamed of her. When, for example, there were newcomers at the Sunday School where her father taught a Bible class, she would walk home with her uncle, without explaining to him the reason for this particular favor of her company. But it happened one day that she and her father were both in the neighboring town of Freeport, where he had been attending a formal meeting at the bank of which he had come to be the head. She watched him walk out on the steps, and he, seeing her below, took off his shining silk hat and made her a low, ceremonious bow. That single gesture destroyed in a moment the false idea which she had been cherishing so long, that he could be ashamed of her. She realized that it was absurd and gladly put it behind her. But those early years of feeling herself lacking in the sturdy well-being of other children gave her a humbleness of mind which she was never to outgrow.

She was six when she went one day with her father on a business errand of his to a mill town not far away. She had not before seen its poorer quarter, into which they now went. The comfortable village of Cedarville did not afford anything so dingy and unlovely. She asked her father why people lived in such "horrid little houses" built so close together. He explained to her that they did so by necessity and not at all of their own choice.

She declared that when she grew up — that magical time to which every child looks forward — she was going to have a large house, not among other large houses, but in the middle of "horrid little houses" like these. And she added that children who had no chance to play at home "could come and play in my yard." It is not often that a young person knows so definitely what she wants to do and proceeds, in the end, to do it. But for the time being just happy playing was one of her most important occupations.

Jane's two sisters were so much older, and were so soon both married, that she might have had a lonely childhood if it had not been for George Haldeman. When Jane was seven her father was remarried to a widow, a Mrs. Haldeman from Freeport. She brought into the family her two sons, Harry who was eighteen and setting out on the study

Jane Addams at six

of medicine, and George who was six months younger than Jane. These two became at once inseparable companions.

Her father's gristmill was a magnificent place to play in when the two were still very young; to keep house in the big empty grain bins or to peer down at the cold dark waterwheel splashing below the floor. When they were a little older it was the sawmill which fascinated them, with the dangerous game of riding on the saw-logs moving up into place and jumping off just in time as they approached the screaming saw. As they grew older still they began to compose the long and intricate games that went from week to week or even month to month, taken from their history books and their reading, in which George was the Knight of the Green Plume and Jane was everybody else. They had plenty of material, for both were eager readers, Jane a truly tireless one.

Her father had told her of how, when he was an apprentice back in Pennsylvania, he used to have to get up at three o'clock in the morning to do his share of watching over the mill and the great turning wheel. There was not a great deal to do so he could read, and he had set himself the task of going through all the books in the little library of the small village where his master had his mills. Jane undertook to do the same and to read steadily through all the books on her father's shelves. Waking up briefly at the same hour became a lifelong habit with John Addams and so greatly did Jane desire to be like him in every way possible that she also took to waking at the same dark and early moment.

She went determinedly through Pope's translations of the *Iliad* and Dryden's rendering of the *Aeneid*. She found this material a little heavy for seven- and eight-year-old reading and finally settled for a *History of the World* as something easier. Her father's advice and incentive gave her some guidance in the matter of her reading; he paid her five cents a life for getting through Plutarch's *Lives of the Greeks and Romans,* and twenty-five cents a volume for Washington Irving's *Life of George Washington* in five volumes. There were few easy or specially edited juvenile books for her.

But both she and George had fertile imaginations, and they invented games of every sort, full of the romantic details of adventure with which Jane's mind was always overflowing. They were both eagerly responsive to that wide green world framed by a busy stream and the lands beyond it, in which they were free to play to their heart's content. Back from Cedar Creek, where the ground settles once more into wide levels, were the cornfields, where long green blades flashed like swords in the summer sun or acres of wheat showed the green ripples of wind patterns. Above them was the great stretch of open sky that belongs to the prairie country. Cedar Creek in the quiet waters of summer and autumn reflected the white flowering thickets of black-berry bushes or the carpets of yellow wild sunflowers. In the spring it went rushing and tumbling down to the Rock River, while the drooping redbud trees hung over it, shedding purplish pink blossoms to be carried swiftly away by the hurrying water. Back from its immediate shores, on the slopes of the hills beside it, the drifting pink of wild crabapple blossoms made a garden of the rough ground. The orchard which John Addams had planted next to his house was a sheet of deep rose blossoms opening to white as the spring days went by. High overhead the honking Canada geese would stream across the sky in spring and autumn. Clarion-throated swans would rise, after brief rest, to their thousand-mile flights to or from the Arctic Circle.

The two children loved all this beauty that lay around them. They looked breathlessly in the spring for the first pale bloodroots and the anemones bowing so lightly to the wind. In the autumn they had a little harvest festival of their own for which they built an altar out of flat stones gathered from the creek and laid upon it one out of every hundred of the green-sheathed walnuts gathered to be dried for the winter. Fresh from the reading of old Greek legends, they poured over them an offering of a pitcher of the fresh cider that was being made in the big barn. Years after, Jane would go over those hours of play in her mind and feel her heart wrung by the thought of what the boys and girls around her were missing, growing up in a crowded city slum.

Jane's absorbing affection for her father and her close companionship with him did not deter her from establishing warm and happy relations with her stepmother. Anna Addams had a great interest in social life, not society as a whole as Jane was to see it, but the Society of formal and informal interchange with one's friends, of dressing well, of polite manners and good living. She had also vigorous intellectual interests which she passed on to the two children now left at home. They would read Shakespeare together, she and Jane and George, sitting around the table of an evening and going through one play after another, each reading a part or parts. For imaginative children it could well make the whole play come alive. Sometimes John Addams could be persuaded to take part also, but more often it was just the three of them. They were, although none of them knew it, simply rehearsing for what was to come even more alive at Hull House later.

Neither Jane's father nor her stepmother had any idea of giving her too sheltered a life or of sparing her the necessity of facing reality; otherwise how could she meet her own difficulties after they themselves were gone? What they taught her in that matter had a severe testing at the time she was fifteen, but no one thought of shielding her from such an experience.

Polly was an old family retainer who had been Jane's early childhood nurse but who had not for some years now been a member of the Addams household. News came one winter day that Polly was seriously ill at the house of some relatives a few miles from Cedarville and was asking to see someone in the Addams family. It turned out that none of the older members were free to go, so it was decided that the duty should fall upon Jane.

She was bundled up and tucked into the robe-filled sleigh which was to take her over the deep-drifted roads. On arriving she was welcomed, warmed and taken up to sit by Polly's bed. After an hour the family left her alone and went down to supper. The big farmhouse room was very cold and still, with no sound except that of the storm beating against the windows. Suddenly she saw that Polly's eyes were fixed upon her face and she heard Polly's feeble voice calling "Sarah," Jane's mother's name. All in a moment Polly was gone, her worn face changing utterly into the serene and unconscious dignity of death.

Jane ran to call the family and presently she was being driven home again through the thickly falling snow and the steadily mounting drifts. Through all the homeward journey she thought of the mystery of death. "Did Polly mind faring forth alone?" she wondered. Or "Would the journey perhaps end in something as familiar and natural to the aged and dying as life was to the young and living?"

She and her father took long counsel together that night,

while his quiet wisdom comforted and reassured her. She was to see death many times later. She was to be many times near to it herself, but it never shook her courage after that night when her father showed her how to look at one of the essential truths of living.

What, in all, did she learn in those free and untroubled early years, from her stepmother, from her father, from the village people about her, from her happiness in the bright and spacious life in which she and George played so energetically? A child who grows up in a country village necessarily and unconsciously learns neighborliness. It is taken for granted that people must help one another; a small community can only operate successfully when neighbors offer each other the services that professional workers perform elsewhere. And there is more in knowing how to be neighborly than simply going to the assistance of others in need. There is the ability to take note of other people's wants of which they themselves more often than not are unwilling to speak, to apply help without hurting sensitive feelings, to accept help without embarrassment, being certain that the occasion for returning the favor is bound to arise in due time. All this give and take in a spirit of wholehearted goodwill Jane saw round about her and accepted without question.

From her stepmother she learned how to face problems in a practical spirit, how to see not only what needed doing but how to get it done. She learned, by indirection, something of greater moment. Anna Addams was a brisk and capable person; she was also determined and very successful in bringing about what she wanted. She had married a man of extraordinary firmness of spirit, who did not make much of exerting authority but who, when necessary, could stand immovable against all comers. Mrs. Addams looked for-ward greatly to those periods when the legislature would be sitting, because the social life of the little capital at Spring-field was something far beyond the scope of small Cedar-ville or larger Freeport. But after two seasons in which John Addams observed the trivial competitions, the little-minded strife involved in the women's activities during the legisla-tive season, he refused to have more of it, and declined reelection to another term of office. His wife was greatly disappointed, and argued long over the question, but she finally saw that she could not change his decision and ceased to attempt doing so. Jane was old enough then to observe firsthand how someone even of strong spirit must recognize the fact of a set idea and bow to the inevitable.

What did Jane learn from her father? She learned, among many others, practical things. She was a good busi-nesswoman when the time came that she needed to be. She inherited from John Addams that innate shrewdness which had made him so successful a businessman, and she was to have need of it all, to the last iota. Beyond such worldly affairs she gained understanding of intangible matters of the inner spirit, through her long consultations with him, for which he was always ready when she needed him. She learned to be patient, as he had had to do. She learned to share his unswerving standards of personal honesty and integrity.

One of those inner impulses that were part of John Addams's character, and which he shared with Jane, was a strongly religious but thoroughly free-thinking spirit. His daughter once asked him "what he was," and realizing just what she meant by that vague question, he replied that he was a Quaker. When she pressed him for further explanation he added that he was a Hicksite Quaker, and would go no further. He went by turns to different churches in the village, gave support to them all, but never became an official member of any one. He had a Bible class, largely attended, at one of them. Jane went faithfully with him every Sunday to be taught, with other, younger boys and girls, what it means to live a Christian life.

There was one Sunday morning when, ready for church-going, she came to show herself to her father, dressed in a new coat which she was impatient to show to the small members of her own class. Her father commented that it was a very pretty cloak but he suggested that she not wear it to Sunday School. It would make the other children feel bad, he said, since they did not have anything like it. She was surprised, but agreed, and pondered the matter carefully as, dressed in her old cloak, she walked beside him to the church.

When they reached the door she stopped him with a question, "Why don't the other children have good new cloaks like mine?"

Her father explained, as he had done before, that some families did not have enough money for all the things they wanted. Jane was not satisfied. "Then what can be done about it?" she demanded.

That was too large a question to be answered on the church doorstep, so they went in together without settling the matter. In fact John Addams could not muster an appropriate reply. Jane was to spend her life seeking for an answer, nor would she give up when it proved so hard to find.

II

Rockford

One of the cherished traditions of the Cedarville community was Old Settlers' Day, with a holiday for all the workers, innumerable picnics in the grove beyond the Addams mills, peanut and sarsaparilla stands, flags and bunting and brass bands. There were patriotic speakers, with John Addams in great demand as one of them. There was frequent mention, to tumultuous applause, of the name of Abraham Lincoln as Illinois' great contribution to history. Young Jane and George always enjoyed these occasions thoroughly, with the cheery noise, the thumping music and the often thrillingly moving oratory. Older persons would recount again their adventures as they and their families had come pressing into that still unsettled region when the country was new and the Indians were dark and unpredictable neighbors.

The generation to which John Addams belonged was the next one after that of the actual pioneers, who had come into this section of northern Illinois thirty years earlier. Young men were now doing what Addams and his bride had done, turning their backs on the old oversafe manner of living which had satisfied their elders, and going forward to seek a new life in more alluring places. The pioneering impulse dwells long in the blood. One can still attribute to it the restlessness of young people who have inherited that same spirit that brought the first settlers to New England and Virginia and that carried them westward, generation after generation. One might think that such instinct for pioneering must die out when all the direct discoveries have been made and all the obvious paths have been explored and well trodden. But the adventures of the spirit go on and on, nor will there be an end of the people who seek them. There can be no doubt that the same spirit dwelt strong within John Addams's daughter and led her to go valiantly into a new way of living for herself and for countless other people.

Jane and George went to the village school which was just across the creek from the Addams house. Jane tended to like best the studies in Latin and English, but George, who was to develop a brilliantly scientific mind, turned eagerly to nature study and biology. Jane's natural impulse for sharing whatever he did drew her to scientific interests also, and she began to form plans to study medicine as he intended to do. His brother Harry, already a surgeon of bold and daring skill, was launched on a distinguished career. He and Jane's older sister Alice had fallen tumultuously in love. Their elders resisted the idea of their marrying, feeling that their two very positive natures were not temperamentally suited to each other. Remonstrance was of no effect, however, and these two were married eight years after Harry's mother had become Mrs. John Addams.

The well-nigh perfect background for a deeply thoughtful child's growing up could not be sufficient for Jane's needs indefinitely, nor for George's. The village school had presently done all that was in its power for this pair of enterprising children and they reached the time of necessary separation. Jane was to go to Rockford Female Seminary and George to Beloit College, neither very far away from Cedarville.

It was Jane's great desire to be a "college woman" and to feel the support and reassurance of a college degree. She had selected Smith College as her coveted goal, and after she and George had come to the end of the Cedarville school's resources, she managed to pass the examinations for entering Smith. That in itself was no mean feat, for small country schools did not often carry their students very far along the path that led to higher education.

One of the greatest disappointments of Jane's early years came when the question of where she should go to college was finally settled. Her father had inexorably fixed on the plan that she was to follow where her sisters Mary and Alice had been sent before her, and where he was a trustee. Yet Rockford, the place of his choice, was not even a college!

It was his idea that such instruction as was obtainable in a small institution like this, to be followed by a year or two abroad studying European art and culture, was the best education for a young woman. Nothing would change that opinion and his final word was law with Jane. The real strength of her character was first shown by the way she conducted herself at Rockford and eventually became, very much through her own effort, a college woman after all. She did not alter her aim; it was Rockford Female Seminary that was obliged to give way.

Jane entered Rockford Seminary in the autumn of 1877. At home she had not had many playmates, since George's company had been happily sufficient. She adapted herself quickly to the hitherto unknown luxury of having all at once a host of friends. Everyone liked her. She was still frail, she still had many backaches. A doctor had once recommended horseback riding as a possible cure, but she herself found it of rather less than any help. Her father had arranged to have her ride every day, nor did she protest, for it would have been of little use.

She has been described by people who knew her in those college years as being slight, with light brown hair, "put up" now, and with an eager, responsive face. She was well dressed, her stepmother insisted upon that. In manner she was reserved rather than shy; she was full of thoughts and strong feelings which, at this stage of her life, she did not attempt to put into words. In intellectual matters she showed immediately a quickness of interest and a penetrating quality of independent reasoning. She followed the usual curriculum of the time, Latin, Greek and French, history, literature, and what seemed to appeal to her most, "Mental and Moral Philosophy."

Rockford Seminary took pride in its standards of study, which were based on those of Mount Holyoke College. This older institution had begun as a seminary but had advanced into administering higher education. There was a possibility of Rockford's also becoming a college, but it did not seem very close. Its charter provided for its giving A.B. degrees when its schedules of study had reached the required higher level. But no official steps were being taken to bring that about, even though a good number of the faculty desired it, as did some few of the students. The principal, Miss Sill, seemed to have small interest in the matter. The goals which she desired to reach were somewhat different and occupied the whole of her absorbed attention.

Jane's natural impulse when a problem arose, as we have said, was to ask at once, "What should be done about it?"

She undertook now on her own initiative to be fully ready for the first moment when the conferring of degrees would be considered possible. She and a friend, Catherine Waugh, registered for courses in higher mathematics and extended their studies in Greek and Latin in order to be prepared to reach the goal of their desires when the time came, and be able to call themselves "college women."

As she followed the stiff course which she had set herself, her active mind turned toward forming her own philosophy. One of the few documents surviving from this period is a little notebook in which she copied down the quotations that most appealed to her. "Always do what you are afraid to do" was a policy laid down from the beginning. There is evidence that her mind was forming the ideals which she, within herself, felt best capable of carrying out. She was also becoming convinced that the exercise of patience and tolerance was one of the best ways of reaching a desired end. She brought a very able mind to the task which she and Catherine Waugh had set themselves. She was to prove that she was one of those eminently capable persons who can do a number of different things supremely well, seemingly without any great effort.

However, it is to be remembered that she was only seventeen when she first entered the school and was no paragon of adult wisdom. She was, in fact, still inexperienced enough to succumb to a certain amount of schoolgirl folly. It was not long before she found herself, with a group of friends, in difficulty with authority.

It came about through too earnest a study of the works of De Quincey in a course in English literature. She and four others had been so carried away by the descriptions in his *Dreams* that they decided to seek some apparitions and visions of their own, summoned, as he had summoned them, by opium. Where they got the drug has not been explained, but it was procured somehow "in small paper packages." These they consumed little by little during a long day's holiday. They waited impatiently for results, but none came. They were much too excited to go to sleep and so failed utterly to conjure up any poetic dreams. Finally they became alarmed and consulted one of the younger teachers, who immediately applied harsh measures. She administered an emetic all around and insisted that no matter how sick they felt they must appear at the hour of evening prayer "whether they were able to or not." Those weird fields of visionary experience which they had hoped to explore were never to come within their reach.

In spite of this unrewarding venture into psychological experiment, Jane began at once to do distinguished work. She stood high in her classes, often at the head of them. Outside of classes, also, she was respected and admired and rapidly became notably popular. Her room was always full of people, talk and activity. Every moment of the day was crowded with intensive occupation of one kind and another. Quite soon she emerged as a spirited and ardent debater and was presently chosen, with Annie Sidwell as alternate, to appear at the Interstate Oratorical Contest at Jacksonville, Illinois.

This was considered to be a very important occasion for

the school. Not only was it an honor for Rockford to be invited to take part in the contest; it was notable that women students had been permitted to compete. Rockford Seminary was already seething with the new campaign for the vote for women, and here was an opportunity to put women on the map. Jane felt very keenly the responsibility resting upon her, "not only for one school but for women in general," as she put it.

Among the competitors was a young man from Illinois College named William Jennings Bryan, of whom the world was to hear more later. The representative from Beloit was not George Haldeman but a friend of his, Rollin Salisbury, who admired Jane greatly. He used to come with George to Rockford for the carefully chaperoned visits which were allowed to the young men from the neighboring college. When the contest was over and the final judging was complete, both Bryan and Salisbury outranked Jane, although neither of them received the prize. Jane, as she said, "stood in the dreary middle," nor did she seem at all cast down by the fact, since she considered the choice of the judges to be eminently right. She persuaded Annie Sidwell, her alternate, to stay on for two days to go with her to visit the two state institutes in Jacksonville, one for the blind, the other for the deaf and dumb.

On their return to Rockford, they were not very happily received, for their friends had been so sure of the success of their candidate that they had prepared a gala and triumphant welcome for them. After the bad news of the final results and the two days of waiting, the carefully planned ceremony fell rather flat. Later Annie Sidwell would be a teacher of the blind for many years. Jane had been very nervous before the debate opened but she had shown at this early date that she had the courage "to do what you are afraid to do" and also that she could nonchalantly see desired success go to another.

In such spare moments as she could find, she busied herself writing articles for the *Rockford Seminary Magazine,* of which she was editor in her senior year. Her writing was very thoughtful and at times rather heavy going, although now and then she struck off a spark of rebellious protest against some routine convention. Within herself she was deeply serious-minded; she had cherished ideals and beliefs which she shared with very few, even in the intimate talks on all the affairs of the universe which are part of college life and a good portion of its profit. But she could be lighthearted and even irresponsible with the rest of her friends on occasion, as they all moved together, full of genuine affection for one another, toward their nearest visible goal — the completion of their education.

Material life at Rockford, as at any college of this period, was indeed spartan. The rooms were bare of anything but the most essential furnishings; students rented a carpet from the school and brought all their personal necessities; they also provided their own bedding. Each girl was required to furnish her own teaspoon. Each room contained a wood-burning stove and roommates took turns getting up first to make the fire. Here at the edge of the prairie country, winds that swept across a thousand miles or so of snow-covered plains could bring the temperature down to ten, infrequently to twenty or even thirty below zero.

There were, of course, no electric lights; night study was in the glow of the "student lamp" with its reservoir of kerosene set low to make it a little less dangerous. One wonders why half the educational establishments in the country did not burn to the ground with so many sleepy students blowing out the lights as they went to bed. But everyone, boys and girls alike, learned how to start and tend a fire as skillfully as Boy Scouts of today are taught to do. Students made their own beds and cleaned their own rooms. On Saturdays George Haldeman, Rollin Salisbury and other swains came over from Beloit, and were even permitted to take the Rockford girls out on sleigh rides, duly chaperoned.

As her college life progressed, it became apparent that Jane Addams had a rare, steady and sincere gift for friendship. A most important quality, it proved to be most especially so for her. A large measure of her success in the work she undertook was due to the friends that she made and cherished through the years. Two of those she met at Rockford were greatly important to her later.

One was Ellen Gates Starr, a girl from nearby Durand, a small Illinois town much like Cedarville. She was a deeply religious girl, with a passion for beauty and all its possibilities in relation to life. She was groping through the strict Presbyterianism of her inherited faith, in search of something that would more truly fulfill her own spiritual needs. She was an eager student of art and wrote articles on it in the college magazine. She and Jane formed a quick and mutually admiring friendship, a thoroughly lasting one even though Ellen stayed at Rockford for only one year and then went away to teach in a fashionable school in Chicago. The two girls carried on vigorous correspondence while they were apart, had visits together at Cedarville and later were traveling companions.

Another of these early friends who played a large part in Jane's life was Julia Lathrop. She had attended Rockford

Seminary for a year just before Jane entered. She left to go
on to Vassar, but her spirited personality was so memorable
that she was invited back to Rockford on all feasible
occasions to aid in theatricals and other affairs of student
activity. Jane's acquaintance with her was a rather casual
one at this time, and was to ripen later.

Jane inevitably attracted to herself young women with
seeking minds like her own, a remarkable group that was
bound together by their personal loyalty to her and by their
staunch belief in what she was doing. And together they
would make social history. Now at Rockford, with good
friends all about her, with the challenge of intellectual
stimulus, aware of growing more mature and wise as the
time passed, Jane would have been well content — except
for one element in the situation: the large and looming
difference between her ideas and ambitions and the intentions of the school's founder and principal, Miss Anna Sill.

That lady, who had been born in Burlington, New York,
had come west to set up a school in true accord with her
own beliefs. She was of a strong religious spirit blended
with a certain amount of intolerance and a great deal of
personal determination. She had intended, during her
growing years, to become a foreign missionary, but discovering that she had special ability as a teacher, she decided
that she would do the missionary cause greater good by
becoming an instructor of young women. Her object was to
train them to be missionaries, or the wives of missionaries,
since the wives needed instruction and dedication as well as
the young men themselves. The missionary boards liked to
send out their emissaries married rather than single and it
was often true that hasty weddings were arranged for those
under new appointment, based more on a likeness of inten-

tions than upon personal feeling or established acquaintance. Beloit had a theological school from which many young missionaries went forth, and Miss Sill had done her satisfied share in supplying able and eligible candidates for such marriages. She readily encouraged the romances that sprang up as a result of the visits and small excursions allowed at the school, seeing them as steps in fulfillment of her own earnest plans. In Jane's time six of the Rockford girls married missionary aspirants from Beloit.

It was inevitable that Miss Sill's practiced eye would observe at once that young Jane Addams was a person of unusual worth and strength of character, just such a one as she would choose to enlist in her missionary purposes. But Jane resisted. She was considered to be one of the "unconverted" girls of the school. "We were the subject of prayer at the daily chapel exercise and the weekly prayer meeting, attendance upon which was obligatory," she says in her reminiscences.

The definite, conscious experience of conversion was something upon which certain people in certain denominations very earnestly relied. Jane had never had it, nor learned to look for it. She had never officially joined any organized church. She had never even been baptized. This was not because of any lack of religious instruction at home nor any lack of innate faith in her own heart. She had simply had a different bringing-up from any Miss Sill was accustomed to, and possessed a different temperament.

Jane's father, to whom she had always turned for counsel about her thoughts and ideas, was, as he had told her, basically a Quaker like his people before him. Quakers do not include baptism in their religious procedure, so that it was nothing out of the way that Jane had not been baptized. Miss Sill, undaunted, set herself to remedy these omissions and errors. It was a very difficult time for Jane. To hear oneself prayed for day after day, even though not by name but before all one's friends, is no happy experience. Members of the faculty, chosen for their posts for their orthodox devoutness as well as for their intellectual attainments, tried to supplement Miss Sill's efforts by persuasions of their own. One of the younger members, of whom Jane was very fond, was especially assiduous, to Jane's great distress.

She knew instinctively that she was not fitted for missionary work, that she was too unorthodox in her beliefs. Further, although her spinal trouble was better at Rockford and she had less pain, she did not have the health that a missionary, or a missionary's wife needed for such a rugged life. She was aware, although it was so far only dimly outlined in her own mind, that she wanted greatly to do good for people of less fortunate position than herself, but she had still no notion of how to go about it. Through affection for George, she had interested herself in scientific studies and had some idea of being a doctor, as he was to be. It would give her a way of reaching the people whom she would want to help, so she thought. And now she realized that she was totally unable to formulate her own religious ideas into any definite creed, or to the canons of any definite church. She had not been taught before that such an act would be considered obligatory.

For some time she spoke to nobody about the struggle which was going on in and about her. It was through her unshaken confidence in her father that she found reassurance when she finally turned to him for comfort and good counsel. One morning in April when she was at home for a brief vacation she at last put before him the truth of what it was costing her to withstand "this evangelical pressure" as she termed it. They were driving together through the woods, green with tiny spring leaves, and they became so absorbed in their discussion that John Addams abandoned any attention to his horses and let them go where they willed. He listened, understood, and forebore to lay down directions or advice.

This was a situation, he told her, that she must deal with herself. For any solution to be final it must be her own. But a person could and should maintain his or her mental integrity above anything else. His words were convincing and strengthening; they gave his daughter infinite relief and a new will to face her difficulties. What John Addams was really telling her was to look for the Quaker "inner light." She found it. The horses, meanwhile, had been taking their own way through the woods, and they were lost.

The weeks of pressure which Miss Sill and others, with the most sincere intentions, had exerted upon her were to stand Jane in good stead. It was a harsh ordeal, this holding so firmly to her own belief and her own integrity; it saddened and upset her and made her uncertain of herself for some time to come. But what she learned from it was perhaps of more avail than anything else that she got from Rockford Seminary.

At the end of her time at Rockford, in the confusion of the graduation period, Rollin Salisbury, George Haldeman's friend, asked her to marry him. What reason she gave for refusing him is not known. The blow seems to have been a bitter one. He never married. He became a distinguished professor at the University of Chicago, but

Jane at the time of her graduation from Rockford

even with Hull House and Jane only a few miles away, he never entered its doors.

Jane was graduated with honors and was chosen to give the valedictorian address at the commencement exercises. She gave Miss Sill a fine and moving tribute which that lady received with dignified countenance. She had had her indirect share in making something unique — namely a Jane Addams. On her own part Jane had come this far in formulating to herself what she meant to do: she was going to "study medicine and live with the poor."

III

Mile End Road

By June of 1882, the year after Jane's graduation, Rockford Seminary declared itself ready to give academic degrees to those who were sufficiently prepared. Jane and Catherine Waugh were the only two who had extended their studies far enough to qualify. They returned at commencement time to become the new college's first Bachelors of Arts — college women at last! The time between the day of Jane's original graduation and this moment of achieving the goal at which she had so long aimed had been a dark and difficult one. She speaks with gratitude of one of her former teachers who had given her comfort and courage "in the black days which followed the death of my father."

For John Addams had died very suddenly in August of that summer, on a journey into Wisconsin which he, Mrs. Addams, Jane and George were taking together. Modern knowledge now recognizes that his death was due to a ruptured appendix, for which there was then nothing to be done. Jane was a person of very deep feelings, of whole-hearted and unwavering affection. This abrupt closing of the years which had been full of such happy trust and understanding between these two, administered a blow that she could scarcely bear. Her father was fifty-nine years old, she was just twenty-one. How could she face all that was to come to her without the support of that warm love, that unfailingly wise counsel which had always been so readily at hand until now?

John Addams left to his wife, who was already well off, to each of his married daughters and to Jane, what was considered then to be a comfortable fortune. The household at Cedarville was now completely broken up. The eldest sister Mary was married to the Cedarville Presbyterian minister; George Haldeman was about to enter the Johns Hopkins Medical School; Mrs. John Addams had always wished to live in a larger and more important place than little Cedarville. Jane herself was anxious to get away. She felt that Cedarville had nothing to offer her now and was impatient to enter the Women's Medical School at Philadelphia and begin her study to be a doctor.

It takes a certain amount of second thought to understand why Jane was so anxious to be a physician, since she had no definite scientific bent. In that plan to "study medicine and live with the poor," the poor were the real factor in the case, rather than the launching of a professional career. But Jane, even though she had been successful, admired and beloved at school, and had almost continuously stood at the head of her classes, was still, as she had always been, completely humble. How did one go about approaching the poor with the object of helping them when one was a stranger to them, with no real right to interfere in their affairs? It is well known that the poor have their own sensitive pride, which they have every right to. Later Jane was able to formulate and speak her conviction that if you want to help poor people you must know them first. But it is equally true that for them to receive your help they must first know you.

She made up her mind that to be a doctor — the right kind of doctor — gave you access at once to the lives and needs of the poor. You would have entrance where people would always be glad to see and trust you, would open their hearts to you. It was true that she had no native bent for medicine such as George Haldeman had in abundance, but she thought that hard work could make up for the difference. She prepared herself by hard study through the summer, passed the examinations and was admitted. She toiled at the medical school from October to April; she did well in her classes — all to no avail.

Her old spinal trouble, which had been in abeyance at Rockford, returned and by spring it was evidently impossible for her to continue her work. She spent some time in Dr. Weir Mitchell's hospital in Philadelphia, and though she does not refer to it in her reminiscences, she must have found comfort and courage in his wise advice and his sustaining presence, as all his patients did. By June she was able, although only hardly so, to go back to Rockford to receive her A.B. degree to which she had so long looked forward. From there she returned to Cedarville but immediately became ill again.

That she constantly missed her father was manifested in a restlessness and a desire to get away from Cedarville, and at last she took refuge with her sister Alice, Mrs. Harry Haldeman, who lived at Mitchelville, Iowa, not far from Des Moines. Her brother-in-law took Jane's case in hand and operated on her spine, and he and Alice watched over

her while she was bedfast for six months. By the summer of
1883 she was able to be up and about, armored by a strait-
jacket of steel and whalebone, desperately uncomfortable
to wear, but which did relieve pain. She kept to it for more
than a year, and after the first mention of it, never spoke of
it again.

Dr. Haldeman had concluded that travel would give her
the relaxation that her tense state needed and distraction
from her continuous grieving for her father. John Addams's old plan of a tour of Europe to supplement her
Rockford training was now revived and it was arranged that
she should go abroad for two years. Her stepmother was to
go with her. By the time plans were completed there were
six in the party. They sailed from New York in August of
1883.

Jane kept a journal of sorts during the journey, since this
was a tour to complete her education. The entries were
scanty in detail except when she had seen something that
had really moved her. What she noticed all along the way
was colored, without her knowing it, by a single interest
overtopping the lesser ones. She observed the pitiful destitution of the people in Ireland and the narrow lives which
they were obliged to live. She knew what workmen got, six
shillings a week ($1.50), while the man whose tenants they
were had a yearly income of £16,000 ($80,000 then). She
was relieved to see model cottages built on another estate,
and the workmen receiving nine shillings a week besides
their houses without rent.

The party made its way through Scotland and northern
England and reached London by late October, where they
settled down for an extended term of conscientious sight-
seeing. There was a Saturday when they journeyed out to

Bethnal Green and came back after dark through London's East End, along the Mile End Road and past the old debtors' prison. The people of the neighborhood were out doing their weekly marketing. Crude gas flares lighted their drawn, anxious faces below as Jane and her friends looked down from the top of their omnibus.

They passed a corner where an auction was being held to dispose of the wilted fruit and vegetables which would not keep until Monday. Near the wheels of their coach one old man had been tossed a rotting cabbage for which he had bid a penny or two. He caught it, sat down on the curb and sunk his face into it, decayed and uncooked as it was, devouring it in wolfish eagerness. The sight was something Jane never forgot — the dark, the flaring lights, the hands — the hands upstretched everywhere in ravenous hunger for the little food which these people could afford. Here were the poor, the real poor, of whom she had so often thought and spoken, without ever fully knowing what real poverty was. Here were people who lived on the ragged edge of existence, their only thought the desperate effort to keep alive. The omnibus lumbered on and the people of the East End disappeared in darkness.

As she declared later, Jane carried away with her a feeling of despair and resentment that poverty like this could be. What was to be done about it? What was she to do? The worst of it all was the knowledge that there was nothing she could do for the moment, if ever, and that furthermore she was not expected to do anything, that her lot was that of the merest bystander. The glimpse of that life which she had caught so briefly was never really to leave her. As she went about London in the following days she would look fearfully down each new street, afraid that she might see such a scene again. And still their plans must go forward, she must go on her way blindly to fill out the two years of the pursuit of culture which her father had planned for her.

A journey abroad at that time was something very different from stepping into a plane, and in less than twenty-four hours arriving at a foreign destination. People who went to Europe remained a year or even two years. Jane studied French in Paris, she passed through miles of picture galleries, saw endless places of interest, filled her journal with pages setting down her impressions. She was not yet fully recovered from her long months of illness and there were weary moments when all that passed before her seemed curiously futile. Finally she and Anna Addams came back to settle for the winter in Baltimore, where George was now an established student at the Johns Hopkins School of Medicine.

Mrs. Addams was anxious to see Jane marry George and he himself was willing indeed, but Jane seemed unable to cooperate. She went about a little in Baltimore society and found it dull. She attended some lectures on archaeology and enjoyed them but knew that they were taking her nowhere. She was all this time far from well and probably on that account was deeply depressed in spirits. She had become dissatisfied with everything, including herself.

She spent the following summer in Cedarville, taking her only pleasure in the company of her sister Mary who lived nearby, and in Mary's children. It was then that she completed a step that she hoped might bring her aid and comfort; she arranged to be baptized and to join the Presbyterian church where Mary's husband was minister. It put an end to the long uncertainty which Miss Sill's misplaced zeal had brought about. She has said of herself that she was beginning to feel a "passionate devotion to democracy" and that the Church, even though varying between denominations, was the symbol of that unity of the spirit which teaches men to act together. Taking this step lightened somewhat the weight of depression under which she had been laboring, but it did not give her the answer to the questions of what was she to make of her life, and how was she to be most truly useful to her fellow men? She has quoted her stepmother and George as asking more than once, "How long are you going to keep on with that philanthropic nonsense?" Just how much influence this had upon her ideas, still vague, concerning a final purpose, is not known. At about this time her father's estate was finally settled, putting her in possession of her own income, whereupon she suddenly decided to go abroad again.

Her love of beautiful things and her interest in historic places were two fields which she could still explore with pleasure. Her school friend Ellen Gates Starr was traveling in Europe at the time and would welcome her as a companion. Jane therefore set forth with another friend, Sarah Anderson, sailing from Hoboken in December of 1887. It took nine days in those years to cross the Atlantic, and December was scarcely a propitious time. Jane certainly did not find it so. But the two arrived safely and proceeded to Paris, from where Jane went on alone to Munich.

She stopped on the way to see the cathedral at Ulm and found in its magnificent proportions and the symbolism of its carvings and windows that uplifting satisfaction in beauty that she had come to seek. That night she spent hours over her journal trying to describe what she had envisioned as a "cathedral of humanity . . . spacious enough to house a fellowship of common purpose." Her seeking mind was beginning to come broad awake, but her ideas were still too large to be fitted into any practical pattern of ordinary life.

The party of three went on to Rome. One of Jane's first visits was to the Catacombs, those dark caves under the city where in the heroic age of early Christianity the faithful believers gathered in secret to hear the words of Saint Peter and hear the reading of the written messages of Saint Paul. The result of the tour for Jane was a bad attack of sciatic rheumatism which kept her in bed for two weeks while the others, at her insistence, went on without her. When they returned she was better, and they all, five of them now, proceeded to Madrid.

Every traveler to Spain feels obliged to see at least one bullfight. The young ladies from America felt that they must do the same. The other four had enough almost at once, but Jane stayed on. She was captivated by the scene of the huge, gaily dressed audience, by the scarves and fans and mantillas, by the intent faces all turned in the same direction. She paid much less attention to the richly costumed matador and to the mortal danger in which he stood to face the furiously charging bull. Thoughts were racing through her mind, still going over and over the question which she was always asking herself: What should she do? How was she to do something for people — great numbers of people like this crowd around her?

She came to herself with a start, realizing that she had been so intent on her own thoughts that much time had passed while she had not heeded the shouts, the trampling hoofs and the swift movement in the arena below. Her friends must have been waiting for her for a long time. She got up and went out hastily to meet their reproaches. She could not offer any excuse for herself. It was after she got back to the hotel and was thinking over the events of a crowded day that real revulsion overwhelmed her. What was she, Jane Addams, doing going aimlessly up and down the world, looking for beauty, for interest and entertainment, sinking all her attention merely in new places and new scenes like that which she had witnessed today? She could go on doing this for years and where would it end? Nowhere, nowhere at all!

At this moment of self-questioning there came to her mind that idea of long ago which she had told as best she could to her father, that she wanted to have a "big house among horrid little houses" and be a friend to those who lived in them. She had tried since then to make many elaborate plans, but she returned now to the one that was so simple, and was after all the best. If she was to carry it out while she was still young enough to give her life to it, the time was now. She turned to Ellen Starr and began trying to explain to her what she had been thinking.

If Ellen Starr had been other than she was, if she had responded differently when Jane shared her thoughts with her friend, even then this exciting idea might have fallen to the ground. Jane, who had an unusual capacity for putting herself in another person's place and imagining what that person was thinking, realized now how foolish all this might sound, how artlessly impractical. But Ellen Starr caught fire at once. It was a splendid, a noble idea and she immediately asked to have part in it. What were they to do first?

The first and most important moment in the history of Jane's purpose was that instant of seeing, in the Mile End

Road, the huge and dangerous fact of real poverty. It was in London that she first had this realization, it was to London that she turned now. Ellen Starr felt that to carry out what she envisioned as her part in the new plan she ought first to see more of Italy, so she prepared to go there, while Jane set her face toward London. After these immediate errands were fulfilled they would go home.

On her first visit to London, Jane had heard reports concerning a group of young men, most of them associated with Oxford, who were making attempts to meet the same problem which so occupied her mind. But she had paid little attention to them, being so involved in the set plan of the journey with her stepmother. She was an experienced traveler now and knew how to find the places and the people that she desired to see. She lost no time when she arrived in London, made a few inquiries here and there, and so, with little delay and armed with a letter of introduction, she sought out Canon Barnett. He was only a bare acquaintance so far, but he and his wife were to be among the warmest and most helpful of friends and supporters.

When Samuel Barnett had earlier been graduated from Christ Church College, Oxford, and had gone on to take holy orders, he had been offered a post close by the college which he loved. Instead he became vicar of the little parish of St. Jude's in London's East End, in the district of Whitechapel. He was invited to address a great meeting at Balliol College, part of Oxford University, and spoke with impassioned fervor of the piteous condition of the packed and impoverished people of his neighborhood, "who live without knowledge and without hope."

A group of young Oxford men were deeply stirred by what he said. They decided among themselves that they would go to live in Samuel Barnett's district, no matter whether they had preparation or training for what they hoped to do. A short time before, a young Oxford man whom they all loved and admired, Arnold Toynbee (father of a great historian of our own time), had died, plainly worn out by his desperately hard work for the relief of London's poor. They would call the place where they lived and did their work Toynbee Hall. They persuaded Samuel Barnett to be the head of their association, giving him the title of warden. He himself insisted that there should be no announced program for social reform, and no sense of self-sacrifice. This was simply to be a new and wiser way of living. It was, in effect, the first social settlement.

Here Jane Addams found young people like herself doing what she so greatly desired to do. They could tell her of possibilities and the difficulties, of what they had accomplished and where they had been obliged to take further thought and try again. She began to hope that she could persuade college women who had not yet learned what to make of their lives to enlist in some work like this, rather than the endless and profitless round of pleasure-seeking that was their usual lot.

At this time there were no schools to train for what we now call social work, to prepare young people for what has become a profession instead of a casually chosen calling. Jane set out to learn all that she could from Samuel Barnett and his helpers. Barnett was firmly advancing the idea that there must be "requisite knowledge" behind every effort to improve, even by a little, the despairing lives of these suffering people. Great and harmful mistakes could be made, he declared, even by persons with the best will in the world, if they put forward well-meaning effort in the wrong way. He was to rise in the offices of the church to become Canon Barnett, and he was to be Jane's friend and adviser for life. Toynbee Hall was her model, not as something to be exactly imitated but as a place where people like herself were learning by experience the things that she must learn. With as little loss of time as possible, she and Ellen Starr hastened home.

There was no question in either of their minds of where the seat of their efforts was to be. Chicago was the nearest large city, thriving, bustling, growing rapidly, full of large prosperity and hopeless penury side by side. It took them some discouraging months, however, to find just the place to make a beginning. There were plenty of "horrid little houses" in truth, as the narrow, dirty little tenements of the West Side undoubtedly were, but where was the big house that would suit their purpose? They had no possible access at that time to funds sufficient for building one, as Toynbee Hall had been built. Months passed and they had found nothing.

They came upon it at last and very much by accident. Jane was driving with a friend to an appointment on Halstead Street on a spring Sunday afternoon. She suddenly caught sight of a "fine old house" as she describes it, with a broad piazza and a gracious space between it and the street. She could not stop then but next day hurried back to seek it out, only to discover that she had been mistaken in its situation and it was not to be found. Even though she searched for several days she did not come upon it again and finally abandoned hope. Three weeks later she and a group of advisers, one of them an ex-mayor of Chicago, had decided at least in what district their location should be. She went to make a thorough inspection of the neighborhood chosen and there, to her delight, she found the big old house again, with its broad porch, its Corinthian pillars and its dormer window extending over the front door.

Inquiry revealed that it had been built forty years before by a successful real estate dealer, Charles Hull. He had meant it to be a suburban residence for himself, but other ventures had prevented his settling there to live. He had become interested in the project of building proper homes for people of moderate means, then later he moved south to provide decent housing for working people, white and black alike, in Maryland, Georgia and Florida, a project very little considered by real estate operators of his time.

He had died not long before Jane and Ellen Starr began their search. Having no children, Charles Hull had left the property, which covered a whole block, to his niece, Miss Helen Culver, who had been his secretary. The two had no difficulty in finding her and in getting permission to examine the house. They entered on an excited tour to see what it was like inside.

It was dirty and littered, having been long uninhabited, and was at the time being used as a storage place by the factory which had been built behind it. But nothing could conceal its fine proportions and dignified spaciousness. A long hall ran through the middle of it, on one side a stately high-ceilinged drawing room, with long windows, fine woodwork, a molded ceiling, and a carved marble fireplace. There was a beautiful dining room, with white paneling and Spanish wrought-iron chandeliers; there was a library of the same proportions as the other generously sized rooms. The rooms upstairs were equally spacious with a good number of fireplaces. The bedroom above the front door,

with the extra space provided by the dormer window, was
eight-sided.

The two young women could not think of buying the
house and most of the lower floor was still under lease. But
they succeeded in renting the great drawing room and the
rooms upstairs. Miss Culver was immediately interested in
their purpose and was warmly cooperative as they made
their arrangements. There was much scrubbing and clean-
ing and painting to be done and much clearing away of old
rubbish. The big house seemed to respond happily as more
and more of its grace and dignity was revealed.

Families and friends of Jane and Ellen contributed furniture out of their own households. There had been a recent
change in fashion of household effects, bringing in a style
of fussy late Victorian taste, with a good deal of fine old
mahogany relegated to attics. To this the house fell heir, to
their great advantage, for it belonged to the period when
the place was built. What they were able to buy was carefully chosen to suit the same era. "Perhaps no young
matron ever placed her own things in her own house with
more pleasure than we did," Jane records.

There was no thought of giving it a fanciful or farfetched
name. Charles Hull had built it and his was to be the
credit; Hull House it was to be. Jane, Ellen Starr, and a
housekeeper, Mary Keyser, who was a friend of one of
Jane's sisters, moved in. The place was opened September
14, 1889. There was no doubt that the old house would
worthily fulfill its new office, although Jane and Ellen
could scarcely predict that before its first year was out Hull
House would receive fifty thousand visitors.

Jane in 1888 when she went to Toynbee Hall

Hull House in 1962

Jane Addams in the year following the opening of Hull House

IV

Living with the Poor

It was the custom in Chicago at that time for families, rich or poor, to sit outside on warm summer evenings on their porches or, lacking them, on their front steps, with a rug laid down and cushions spread, to greet friends and neighbors who strolled past. Mid-September was still warm summer for the Middle West, and on that first Sunday night, four days after moving in, Jane Addams, Ellen Gates Starr and Mary Keyser were sitting on Mr. Charles Hull's broad piazza and, like thousands of others, viewing the world of Halstead Street as it passed slowly by. It must have been practically the first time they had sat down since moving day.

The whole community was seething with curiosity regarding these ladies, who could so well afford to live elsewhere, and who had so surprisingly come to share the atmosphere and surroundings of a city slum. Various people went by, eyeing the big house now reopened in a new guise. Presently a group of very young boys and girls hesitated, took note of the smiles of warm greeting of the ladies on the porch, and came up the steps. Jane Addams had, among her other gifts, that of being able to make acquaintances easily and to draw people out to talk about themselves. Very soon the small group was seated and the most talkative one of the boys was telling the ladies "about things around here." When Jane led the conversation to himself, his desire and ambitions, he answered readily, in very high-flown language, to tell of just the sort of hero he meant to be. Even the girls, when pressed, admitted to dreams of highly colored romance. Jane would realize later that this sort of language was almost directly lifted from the plays they had seen in the cheap theaters of which the neighborhood was full. There were no movies then, but these theaters — entrance fee five cents — filled the same need. "Going to the show" was the only stimulus their imaginations received in the bare, monotonous lives they were obliged to live, but their fancies could run riot, and did.

Visitors from the neighborhood began coming immediately and in numbers in those first days, some inquisitive, some suspicious — "What do these women want from us?" — some eager to be friendly and cooperative. "If these strangers want to know about us, we'll tell them" seemed to be the prevailing sentiment. Miss Addams would open the door herself, would ask them in for a cup of tea, and while they drank it, sitting timidly on the edges of their chairs, they would find themselves presently telling about their homes, their families and their problems. It was among those early acquaintances that Jane made her first quite terrible blunder.

In the first rather haphazard day nursery that almost at once came into being at Hull House, a baby had been left unclaimed. Investigation through the police revealed that it had been born ten days before at the great Cook County Hospital not far away, and that no trace could be found of the mother who had deserted it. The little thing proved to be very delicate but it was cared for with the greatest attention and affection. A trained nurse was secured and the best child doctor in Chicago was brought by Jane to try to save it. Measures for rescuing sick babies were scantier in those days than they are now, and in spite of all effort the poor little deserted thing lingered only a few weeks and then died. The neighborhood knew all about the affair at once, for all the neighbors knew each other well and told one another everything. Immediately Jane was waited on by a half-dozen of her new acquaintances. What were the — the arrangements being made for burial, they asked. Miss Addams said that because the settlement had carried the considerable expense of the baby's care up to now, it was time for the county to come into the picture, since there was provision made for the burial of the friendless at public cost.

The women received her answer with horror. No, no, that would never do, a county funeral, a pauper's grave? It was the thing that above all others every one of them dreaded. In all their poverty they had taken up a collection; they would see to the funeral for this little waif whom they had not known or seen but who had died among them. Yet they understood, they assured Jane Addams, that she could not have known what she was doing. She and Miss Starr were single ladies and so "could not know a mother's heart." Jane realized at once what a mistake she had made and was quick to learn from it. She never made such a one again.

Jane Addams had always lived in a country town. She knew nothing of city living in any walk of life. Ellen Starr, who as has been said taught for a time in a fashionable girls' school on the prosperous North Side of Chicago, still knew nothing of what it meant to live on Halstead Street. It was worlds away from anything either of them had ever known or even imagined. What they were to find was astonishingly pitiful, some of it terrifying, some of it heartwarming. They both knew that they were plunging into a flood of new experiences whose depths they could have no way of measuring. But neither of them was dismayed. They were both able to realize how much they did not know, and both were completely ready to learn. The main thing was to make a beginning. One wonders why they were not, at the first experiences, bitterly discouraged.

But to them there was really no temptation to lose heart and turn back. What carried them forward in the midst of such a vast scene of destitution was the fact, evident above everything, that they were needed. The smallest children, left alone every day by their employed mothers, soon made it clear that the ladies of Hull House were needed. The half-grown boys lounging on the street corners after school needed them. The bewildered young people just grown to early maturity and entering such a hurried and unheeding world needed them. The newly married — all neighbors alike — were in want of what Hull House was ready to offer. Beyond all these was that army of toilers, among them some very old, some cruelly young, working in the factories and shops, both themselves and their employers clutched in a harsh industrial system from which neither could see means of escape. For these there seemed at first little that Hull House could do, but even that little might serve to make those toiling lives somewhat less appallingly dreary.

Arrangements came first for the small tots whose mothers went to work, locking them in during the winter or locking them out in summer when the tiny tenement rooms would become too stiflingly hot to bear. It was impossible to leave doors open lest the whole contents of the place be stolen. To get away from the merciless heat the smallest ones took to wandering over to Hull House, spending the whole day in the long hall which, with its high ceiling, was always pleasantly cool and airy. They were very quiet, knowing that they were there on sufferance. Various people of the house who could find the time would keep an eye on them and see that they got some lunch at midday, but the small visitors asked for little. In a short time there grew to be so many of them that some more definite arrangement had to be made for their regular care. And in more time a nearby cottage was found, relic of the West Side's better days, where a permanent day nursery was set up.

Payment for the services there was voluntary, but various children would arrive at Hull House with a penny, hot from being clutched in a small hand, to be paid for the food, shelter and cordial affection which were so readily available. In more time still the Children's Building as a further part of the Hull House complex was donated for their special needs. So, out of this group who found Hull House for themselves and adopted it as their chosen haven, grew the day nursery, where mothers, winter and summer, could leave their children in comfort and safety and, a rare thing until then, in happiness.

Very soon after the day nursery there came the kinder-

garten. Jenny Dow was the first of the volunteer workers
who arrived to help at Hull House, a very young girl with a
genius for understanding children and drawing them out.
Her gaiety, her visible delight in living in all its aspects,
affected the whole atmosphere of Hull House, for no one
could be downhearted when she was nearby. She was small,
very pretty, full of overflowing good spirits. One of the
greatest tributes to her came when it was presently discovered that the children all thought that she was the same
age as themselves, "a little girl in a white apron."

The kindergarten was her idea and in her charge from
the very first. There was never any question concerning its
immediate and full success. She taught the children to
march and sing together, to make things of paper and clay,
how to play together in comfortable peace, how to open
their hearts to the light that was coming into their bare
little lives. She made the children happy through every
hour of the kindergarten day. She left after two years to be
married and died tragically soon, leaving little children. Jane
Addams spoke of her spirit as "like a flame."

The medium-sized girls were not quite so easy to provide
for, but presently they had their own clubs, their cooking
lessons and their sewing classes where they could dress dolls
or later sew for themselves and chatter unendingly with a
dozen or so similarly busy companions.

The boys presented probably the most complex problem
of all. Jane thought often of her own playtime with George
for a companion, and how far distant it was from the background of these urchins who spent their time after school
in the street finding amusement as best they could. Their
games never could be continuous or complete because of
the constant interruption by traffic or by unsympathetic

police, and were limited by the myriad windows that balls might break or streetlights which might be damaged. In the end, the boys' amusements usually degenerated into standing idly around on street corners, roughhousing and getting into mischief, to the great annoyance of householders, police and passersby. But now Hull House came to their aid.

Jenny Dow had brought a new volunteer to Hull House, younger than herself, very shy, very anxious to be of use and very able, capable of devoted loyalty, and as life unfolded for her, of a greater and greater quiet wisdom. This was Mary Rozet Smith, daughter of one of Chicago's most well-to-do merchants, brought up in the narrow and exclusive circle of "Chicago's old families" but thirsting to do something of real value with her life. Her situation was much what Jane's had been earlier. The two felt immediately that theirs were kindred spirits, and although Jane was older, they cemented a friendship in their work together that was to last through their whole lives.

Mary Rozet Smith lived at home with her family where her father, after retirement, had become blind and where her mother was an invalid. She was the center and life of her own family but that did not diminish her services to Hull House and her determinations to further the work of Jane Addams in any way she possibly could. She had a quiet fashion of covering deficits, of calming troubled or contending spirits, of doing the thousand odd jobs that a dozen other people had overlooked. Everyone loved her, everyone recognized instantly the strength and the complete generosity of her wise judgments.

She turned her attention at once to the situation of the street boys. She could see, as Jane did, that they must have their recreation in some form or other, but the crowded

Mary Rozet Smith with her niece

streets were poor places for play since baseball was for-
bidden and the policeman on the beat often fielded the
ball and broke up the game. Cops and robbers seemed to
be the only other practical diversion, but this could get
badly entangled with the horse-drawn traffic which filled
the cobbled streets. They did not have the resources to
invent such games as Jane and George used to play; there
could be no chance of imagining oneself to be Bellerophon
taming Pegasus or Hercules destroying the Nemean lion.

Space was made in Hull House for their table games,
their jackstraws, pool and chess. They came to play them
after school and were readily absorbed in them, but they
deserted their games at once when Mary Rozet Smith read
to them or told them stories. Then they listened with en-
chanted attention, for here was something totally new in

[55]

their lives. Their young imaginations took wings; each boy could feel himself capable of great things. By choice they called their group the Young Heroes Club.

Mary Rozet Smith added one more service which no one noticed at the time. During the very brief intervals when she and Jane were not working together at Hull House there was a constant exchange of letters between them. Jane, who did not have a secretary until much later, never kept copies of her letters, especially not of the hasty long-hand notes that went so often to her friend. But Mary Rozet Smith kept every one that she received, to be found in her desk after she died. They are available now in the files of Jane Addams papers preserved at Swarthmore College. Reading them, one becomes better acquainted with Jane Addams herself than would be possible through any recorded description. Many small details of the ups and downs of the excessively active, of the more than excessively successful life at Hull House are here recounted, many acknowledgments of timely gifts, great or small, are gratefully included.

Moreover, one feels in reading them that they are not so much accounts of the crises and necessities of the humming life going on there, but messages between two friends who feel so close that each wishes to share with the other all the small matters of life as they are living it, just as all close friends like to do. This devoted helper rendered a myriad of acts of assistance, unobtrusive checks to cover small deficits, a set of furniture for a newly opened room, an organ; in time a Children's Building was given by Mary Rozet Smith and her family. Jane's letters are unsentimental and matter of fact, but occasionally one will end unexpectedly, "Yours until death." Time was to show that this was undeviatingly true.

Jane Addams was fiercely sure that young persons coming to maturity must have their share of recreation and happiness. Many of them, boys and girls both, went to work at the age of fourteen, and it was like being locked into a prison of a dull ever-repeating job for life. How were they to know one another as they grew up, how to choose wives and husbands? All too many found themselves married to the wrong person having taken the first infatuation for convincing love. Jane could tell many pitiful stories, confided to her by young people who came to her, having no one in their own hard-driven families to whom to turn.

There was a young man who told her of how he fell in love with a girl of sixteen, and since her parents objected to their marriage, had persuaded her to run away and marry him. They were still on their poor little honeymoon when they got to the end of their money, and went into a cheap restaurant to spend their last penny. There he saw an overcoat hanging unguarded and stole it, although his little bride earnestly begged him not to. He went boldly out with it over his arm and was almost immediately arrested. The girl announced that she had also taken part in the theft and they were both thrown into jail to await trial. Only once were they allowed to communicate and she told her young husband what she had decided. If he were put into prison and she was released, she had nowhere to go. She could not go home, she had no source of money. She was, therefore, going to take the whole blame upon herself. She was then barely seventeen.

He protested, but before they came to trial she sent for the district attorney and made full confession of being the only one involved in the crime. As a consequence, her husband was released, weak and bewildered, not knowing what to do. She was convicted and sent to the state prison. When he came to Jane Addams he had just been allowed to see her for the first time. The surroundings were so terrible that he was stricken with terror and remorse; he feared that she was developing tuberculosis. She still insisted that, dreadful as the prison life was, she could bear it for herself but could not bear it for him. There was no juvenile court then, no system of probation or parole. An able probation officer would have quickly got the whole story from her, but then no such person was available. What Jane Addams advised him she does not say, but we can be certain that the counsel was wise.

She speaks also of going into one of the public dance halls to look for a girl she knew, and being accosted by a young man who recognized the friendliness in her smile and who asked her to introduce him to "a nice girl" since he had just come to Chicago and knew absolutely nobody. She told him that he could hardly hope to find a nice girl at such a place. The public dances were got up by saloons, for the sake of the entrance money and the profit from selling drinks. Nice girls did not patronize them.

It was for young people like these that, as space became available, Hull House organized Saturday night dances, unobtrusively chaperoned, serving soft drinks, with good music and a carefully chosen but generously large invitation list.

The day nursery had been brought about by the small children themselves; another organization also came of itself through those who needed it. A group of working girls had been holding a meeting at Hull House to discuss the problems of some friends who were involved in a strike against the poor wages and bad conditions in the shoe factory where they worked. Their demands were steadily refused; they were sure that they would lose their jobs as a penalty for striking, and since they had to live on their earnings, there seemed to be nothing to do but give in. One of the girls at the meeting suggested, "Wouldn't it be fine if we had a boarding club of our own and could stand by each other in a time like this."

With the efficient help of Hull House the plan was quickly realized. Two available apartments were found nearby, with Hull House guaranteeing the rent for the first month. Furniture was contributed or purchased, and the first fifteen girls moved in May 1, 1891. They immediately decided to call themselves the Jane Club. In three years the whole apartment house was filled; the fifteen had become fifty. A little later still talk began over how good it would be "if we could have a building of our own."

One of the prosperous friends of Hull House bestirred himself to seek for means to bring this about. He came to Miss Addams in great delight to say that he had found a donor who would give $20,000, a sum that was ample in those days for the sort of building they needed. But when he told Jane the name of this generous person, the plan collapsed. In some uncanny way Jane Addams always seemed to have the requisite knowledge to bring to bear on any occasion. The man who had offered the money was notorious among the working girls for the meager wages he paid his employees, and the long hours he inflicted on all his working force.

Jane Addams said firmly that they could not take his money.

It was an embarrassing situation for the friend who had

arranged the gift. But she was not to be moved by this fact, entrenched as she was in the firm recognition of what was or was not right. The would-be offer was declined and the man who had made it was left to meditate upon the reason why. Seven years later there came, from another source, a contribution of $15,000 for such a building, which was joyfully added to the group already beginning to surround Hull House.

It was always a special satisfaction to Miss Addams that the Jane Club had been started by the girls' own initiative. They had defined their own wants. They wished above all, as they stated in the beginning, to have some means of helping out their friends and co-workers when they were pressing for needed changes, but were afraid of losing their jobs. They wanted other things also: an opportunity to cooperate on expenses, a place where they could invite and receive their friends, girls and young men together. Girls who were engaged to be married wanted an opportunity to get more fully acquainted with their future husbands. They wanted, besides, some chance to practice housekeeping in preparation for having homes of their own. "I never had a chance to see a meal prepared," one girl declared. Working from seven in the morning to seven at night gave no time at all for real housekeeping. To help with the dishes after an exhausting day in the factory was not an inspiring introduction to the duties of married life.

Other girls outside the Jane Club had difficulties of the same kind. A very young wife came to Jane in tears; her husband had told her that he was going to have to leave her — she was such a bad cook he could no longer stand it. The Hull House evening cooking classes solved her problem; she too had not had any chance before marriage to learn anything of the domestic side of life.

Hull House presently established also its system of residents, making room for those who would live there, even though their means of livelihood was not close by. They would give what spare time they could to those increasing tasks of leadership in the clubs, art classes, dramatics, and a host of other activities. They were not there to study to be "social workers"; the title and the schools for training them were yet to come. But they could not be there and not learn immeasurably from Jane Addams and the brilliant group of leaders that was gathering around her. A great number of young persons who were later to have distinguished careers began as residents at Hull House and went on enriched by what they found there.

At Christmastime in that first year of 1889, Hull House held its first general party. Interest in the place — both on the part of those who needed it and those who were so willing to do their utmost to meet that need — had advanced. Miss Culver, owner of Hull House, had at first given a lease only for what space was immediately available. When she saw what a success Hull House was, she managed to sever all the existing contracts and offered Jane and Ellen Starr the use of the whole house. The great drawing room with its stately proportions, its Christmas decorations and its crowd of chattering laughing guests now came nobly into its own. All those invited arrived and brought others with them. The youngest working girls, the mothers and fathers, the babies that could not be left at home, the old grandparents who could not speak much English but were content to sit and beam at the happy swirling amusements around them — all were there.

So far Jane and Ellen Starr had been attempting to finance their venture out of their own incomes, although it was clear that this could not go on much longer. For this Christmas party Jane had scraped together every penny to provide the presents, the food, the candy and all the other necessities for such a gathering. She was an adroit buyer and could make money go surprisingly far. So she took great pride in buying also, for each member of the Boys Club, a copy of Carl Sandburg's *Abraham Lincoln: The Prairie Years.* Here was a real hero to add to the others of whom their club had been hearing.

There was one unhappy detail. A group of little girls, whom Jane had not seen before but who were brought in late by their families, stood a trifle subdued and aloof. When they were offered the Christmas candies which the others were all enjoying, they diffidently shook their heads. They worked in a candy factory, they said, from seven o'clock in the morning until nine at night, and the very sight of candy was unbearable. Some other kind of refreshment was found for them, but these pale and weary children weighed heavily on Jane's heart in all that tumult of Christmas gaiety, and she could not put them out of her mind, although the party went on to a great success.

Between September when Hull House opened and Christmas, the settlement had already gathered so large a clientèle that one party, in the space available, could not include them all. At New Year's Day there was another gathering for the older people. This was reminiscent of Old Settlers Day, that yearly occasion at Cedarville which Jane had loved when she was a child. The celebration here was very different from that older one with its picnics in the grove, its brass bands and patriotic speeches. But the proneering spirit was there just the same, for many of these older people could remember coming to Chicago when it was no more than a village, could look back cheerily on the hardships of those days, and could recount them to a rising generation meeting its problems in turn. Many of them could give harrowing accounts of the Great Fire, which had burned up almost to the doors of Hull House before a change in the wind spared it. The party was a gay affair with folk dancing and songs of the fatherlands. It would become a tradition at Hull House for the older neighbors to come together there at New Years'. Jane and Ellen Starr could go to bed that night, bone-weary but satisfied that as Halstead Street hostesses they had definitely been accepted. But in Jane's mind there still lingered the troubled memory of those tired, pale little girls who worked fourteen hours a day and could not look at candy.

V

Halstead Street

The surroundings of Hull House were full of children, playing on the broken sidewalks, or when the policeman was not looking, in the badly paved streets. The cobblestones or wooden blocks which made the pavement were worn and broken; it was an interesting game for small fingers to find which ones were loose and pry them out. In summer when there was no school these youngsters were everywhere, cheerful, noisy and ragged. When the big lumbering ice wagon made its way down Halstead Street, it was followed by a line of them, begging the iceman for the chunks and splinters of ice which fell off as the heavy blocks were sawed into halves and quarters. The children would receive the dripping lumps joyfully, crack them on the rim of the wagon wheel into smaller pieces and put them into their mouths to suck. The iceman, standing on the step at the back of the big wagon, would speak to his great heavy horses, who would move on to the next stopping place without need of guiding reins. That sound of ice being sawed was unmistakable and unforgettable; an old person who heard it in childhood would recognize it instantly today.

Another familiar note mingling in the daily pattern of street noises was that of the milkman's bell as he stopped his cart with its two tall milk cans before one house or another and rang his stout handbell. At the signal someone, usually a child, came out with a crock or a pitcher to receive the day's meager supply of milk, and woe betide any small messenger who spilled a drop of it on the way to the house.

On warm summer evenings there was one more familiar sound, equally recognizable and characteristic, when the ice cream man made his rounds in his cart, his foot pressing the bell on the floor to call everyone who had a few pennies to come and be refreshed.

In the mornings when school was in session there would be a period of scampering footsteps and noisy chatter as the children all went off, after which would be a time of comparative peace when only the horse-drawn vehicles passed by and the women went to do their scanty market- ing, women with shawls or kerchiefs on their heads and battered baskets on their arms. In the late afternoon there was an upsurge of high chattering voices again as the chil- dren came trooping home from school, laughing and shouting and chasing one another up the ramshackle wooden outside stairs to their tenement homes above. There were no fire escapes; few houses were connected with the sewers, and for each building the whole water supply was a hydrant at the edge of the street. Once there had been nothing but a squeaking pump; the hydrant was a modern improvement beyond price. It did not, however, make any lighter the buckets to be carried up one, two or three flights of stairs, spilling as they went into worn and broken shoes.

And later in the evening when dusk had fallen on the long summer days, after dark later in the year, the streets were full again, this time with the workers coming home. Most of them were young, many of them children, but there was no laughing and frolicking now, no chatter of young eager tongues. Pale and weary, walking listlessly, they came home together after twelve, fourteen, sometimes even more hours of work since seven o'clock in the morning. They came through the badly lighted streets, swinging their lunch buckets, and climbed heavily up the rickety staircases to their bare and shabby little homes. But there was welcome there and family affection, food prepared and waiting, for families stood firmly by their members, and people in tenements can love as warmly as people in palaces.

In all of their neighbors' domestic matters, Jane Addams and Ellen Starr quickly had their full share of those friendly duties that the rest of the community offered as a matter of course. They washed new babies, they sat up with sick people, they minded children when the mothers were called away. They tried, little by little, to introduce these new friends to some better and wiser ways of living, but this was not a matter so readily acceptable as was help in the drudging duties of daily living. People, especially people who had been born beyond the seas, did not easily change their old household ways even when life in the New World so definitely demanded it. Jane Addams, Ellen Starr and other friends who helped at Hull House all had to learn to be patient.

Among the growing number of residents was a young

woman doctor, Grace Meigs, who by day worked in the Children's Memorial Hospital in another part of Chicago, but who was ready, during the hours she was at Hull House, to respond to neighborhood calls when needed. She has told of how she was summoned at midnight to an emergency some blocks away, and how, following directions, she had to feel her way in the pitch blackness of a narrow unlighted alley — there being no electric flashlights available in that day. She came at last to the door which the message had indicated and which seemed to be the right one. It was unlocked and opened upon an enormous foyer, dimly lit but showing, in spite of the dirt that was everywhere, a vast floor that was paved with marble. Broad staircases went up into darkness where presently lights showed and numberless inquisitive heads peered over the rail.

The place was an old hotel, built like Hull House itself at the time when the West Side was the fashionable quarter of Chicago. Outside it was so swallowed up by adjoining tenements and stables that its original four walls had ceased to be recognizable. No later-coming builder, converting the rooms upstairs into apartments, had known just what to do with that immense floor space so had left it as it was, a witness to the West Side's earlier glories. The place served now, like most of the other West Side buildings, as quarters for several times the number of inhabitants for which it had originally been planned.

That dark cavernous space was a stark reminder of what rapid changes had come to Chicago. Its earlier growth had come because in its situation in the middle of the country at the foot of one of the Great Lakes and surrounded by a maze of eastern and western and southern railroads it was a natural shipping place. Western-grown cattle and lumber were received there and forwarded to the markets of the East, while the manufactures of the eastern states and cotton from the South and imported luxuries from Europe all flooded in to be sent westward. The first prosperity, rapidly seized upon, stemmed from this fact. But as fortunes grew, it was beginning to become a manufacturing city in its own right, producing steel, farm machinery, glass and clothing for the ever-growing markets of a flourishingly prosperous country.

People rejoiced in the magic growth of the city, "a metropolis built in a generation." They admired the millionaires' palaces going up along the North Shore lakefront, the battlemented Potter Palmer castle, along with other huge, luxurious, sometimes beautiful, sometimes hideous dwellings of the successful merchants, bankers and manufacturers that followed one another in dizzily increasing numbers. A fashionable store, advertising a new style of overcoat, declared "every millionaire in the city has one."

Stately houses of better or worse or much worse taste were going up, to the pride and satisfaction of their owners, on the fashionable North Side. On State Street mercantile establishments vied with one another in the magnificence and ornamentation of their expensive storefronts. Satisfied owners went to church on Sunday, the men in tall silk hats, the women in sealskin coats that reached to their heels. All week he had been working at his desk, amassing money; she had been equally busy spending it. They would sing contentedly together, "The heathen in his blindness, Bows down to wood and stone."

But this new and apparently profitable industrial growth, of more or less haphazard character and totally unregulated by law, was not only creating wealth, it was also extending poverty. Business competition was so fierce as to be ruthless; unending watchfulness over expenses and profits was necessary to keep the fortunes which were growing up like mushrooms, but which could vanish almost overnight. The greatest effort, so most manufacturers and other employers thought, must be made to keep costs down. So they spent the least possible amount on working conditions and surroundings for their employees and paid the least possible wages.

Hordes of immigrants were coming in from Europe — from Ireland after a devastating famine, from Germany to escape the long-term and arduous military service, from Russia to flee persecution. With the hard conditions at home, tales from America about the prevalence of jobs there made it seem like a promised land. They did not realize that the difference in the cost of living would mean that what they received would only barely cover a hopelessly narrow subsistence, or not cover it at all. They were so eager for jobs they would snatch at anything. They were shamelessly exploited by unscrupulous employment agents, they fell behind with their rents, they grew poorer and poorer.

Few realized that the industrial conditions in Chicago, changing so rapidly for the better for some, for the worse for others, were growing unendurable and indefensible for the great laboring population. There was little evidence of this along the avenues and boulevards of the North Side, but it was starkly and unavoidably visible in the neighborhood of Halstead Street. It was evident to Jane Addams, who understood that here was a deep-seated and threatening situation which only long-range planning could better.

For the time being all she could do was to attempt to give aid here and there.

There arrived at her door one day a group of girls who worked in a factory near to Hull House. They wanted Miss Addams's advice: their friends and neighbors had begun to look up to her as an unfailing source of kindly wisdom. Perhaps she could do something for them. They were not a union, they had no notion of how to organize a union. They had merely had "a scrap with the foreman" over wages, and what should they do? Jane had heard of Judge Tuley and his Tuley Law, by which disputing parties could have their differences reviewed before him, not in court with lawyers and a jury, but in his own chambers in direct discussion. Both sides in such a procedure were to agree that they would accept whatever the decision of the judge would be.

Jane went with the girls to appear before the judge and noted with appreciation the patience and wisdom with which Judge Tuley listened, questioned, and heard them out. It did not matter that the difficulty was a very small one and concerned only a few cents' difference on their hourly wages. In the end he offered a wise and careful solution for the problem, which both sides readily accepted. When the girls were gone Miss Addams stayed behind to talk to the judge, for he was interested in knowing more about what she was doing at Hull House. He settled himself to hear all about it, and from that time forward he was a firm ally of the settlement, and as the years passed, a great help and support to Jane in many ways.

Besides all her work at Hull House in seeing neighbors and overseeing children, she and Ellen Starr were doing the housework of the big dwelling that was beyond the power of the housekeeper Mary Keyser. No small part of it was sweeping the extensive floors and washing the long windows of the great high-ceilinged rooms. But they managed much beyond all that.

Jane had some friends already in Chicago, Ellen Starr had more, and the two would go everywhere they were invited to talk of Hull House and its intentions: to a group of friends in the parlor of their North Side supporter Mrs. Welmarth, to women's clubs or church groups. They did not ask for money; they were so far only explaining what it was that they were trying to do. People were interested, people wanted to help, people — especially young people — presented themselves at the door of Hull House desiring to be of use.

Part of Jane's excellent executive ability consisted in knowing where prospects of work could be found, and also what charitable organizations existed which could offer relief and help to people in honest need. Hull House had no extensive funds to give away, but it is not to be counted how many people found employment through Jane Addams's tireless efforts in their behalf. This was merely a part of the broadening of her circle of acquaintances among rich and poor and the fact that her experience was being steadily extended, sometimes in rather startling ways.

She awoke once in the darkness of midnight and realized that there was a man in her room. Instead of alarming the house, she fell into conversation with him and under her patient courtesy he took courage to speak out, and she, who was developing a trained ear for truth and falsehood, believed him. He was out of work, he told her, and his family was in such need that he was desperate enough to do anything. She directed him to go out quietly without waking anyone, to be especially careful not to disturb her little nephew asleep in the next room, and to come back at nine the next morning and she would do what she could to find him work. He came accordingly and she found a place for him.

Again and again Jane was to see evidence of what she had learned early, how good the poor were to one another, out of all proportion to what they had. She knew a family living in the narrowest and meanest of quarters who unhesitatingly took in a widow with five children who had been dispossessed. Another instance was that of a young woman whose husband had been sent to prison when she was within three months of having her first baby. By the end of that time, with the baby close to arrival, she was penniless, had been evicted from her apartment for non-payment of rent and had literally no one to whom she had a right to turn. She went to the tenement where an acquaintance lived whom she could scarcely claim to call a friend, since all they had in common was that they had worked in the same factory for a time.

She remembered that this friend — for a friend she surely proved herself to be — had been living in three rooms, but it turned out that the husband had been out of work for some time, so that the three rooms had been reduced to one. Yet they took the girl in without question. At the critical moment when the baby's coming was immediately at hand the husband went off at midnight to find a midwife and was able to persuade her to come, even though he could only promise that she would be paid later. For the next week it was necessary for the husband to sleep on a park bench, but as he commented cheerfully, fortunately it rained on only one night.

A somewhat different occasion was when a woman came to Jane to say that she had been arrested for stealing and selling school books and would Miss Addams just "speak to the judge" to make it all right. The alderman of the ward was away, she said, or she would have gone to him. Were the books really stolen, Jane Addams wanted to know. It was indeed plain that they were, since they were clearly stamped in red as being the property of the school. The woman finally admitted that they were, but that was not the point. The alderman would at once have made everything right, but she was sure that Miss Addams could accomplish the same thing if she would just "speak to the judge." Miss Addams would not, and the woman went away, denouncing Hull House and its head resident as being inexplicably mean and uncooperative.

Three boys who were members of the different clubs at Hull House were hurt, one after another, all by attending the same machine in a factory nearby. A guard appliance that would have done away with the danger would only have cost a few dollars. One boy was so badly injured that he died. Jane went to see what could be done in the matter of getting compensation from the employer. She discovered to her dismay that parents had to sign permission for a child to go to work at the age of fourteen and at the same time had to agree to a release from any claims for damage occurring "through carelessness." Anything, of course, that went wrong was bound to be attributed to a child's carelessness.

In one of her other visits Jane came across a little girl of four sitting on a stool by her mother, pulling out basting threads from the garments her mother was finishing. This was not a mere matter of "helping mother," it was regular employment lasting hour after hour for the whole day. The system of manufacturing garments at that time was to send them out from the factory partly completed, to have the handwork and final touches done at home. The wages were unbelievably small, ten cents a dozen for finishing men's trousers, for instance. Even the little girl should have got that for getting out the bastings, but it was not she who worked for such wages, it was her mother.

The poor mother, forced to work so many hours a day at such miserable wages, could only spare the smallest possible time to buy or prepare food for her family. She would rush out and purchase whatever was nearest at hand and would be the quickest to cook, with no thought of whether it was nourishing or healthful. The places where these garments were finished at home came to be called sweatshops, in reference to the close and stifling rooms where the work went on. The employers who had charge of them were called sweaters.

To meet one difficulty at least, Hull House could make a move. The Coffee Shop was added to the Hull House buildings. Its attractive interior was planned in the likeness of an old English inn. There was a trained director who could give demonstrations of how to cook cheaper cuts of meat and how to prepare a balanced diet with sufficient vegetables and fruits. People could eat there or take out food to give their families at home. But strange to say, at first it was not much of a success. Many preferred their own accustomed ways of cooking and their own familiar kinds of food. It seemed that the Coffee Shop was a discouraging failure; then suddenly it took on new life. Women began dropping in, in parties together to have a bit of gossip and a bit of refreshment at comfortably low prices. The *kaffee-*

klatsch of the Old Country was pleasantly revived here at Hull House. Men began coming too; the place began to be a real rival to the saloon across the street. Jane Addams always insisted that a saloon was the poor man's club, that the majority of its patrons went there for sociability, but one did not hear so much about them, only about the weaker souls who used the saloon for over-drinking.

The changed purpose of the Coffee Shop did not trouble Jane; she was used to unexpected happenings large and small and unexpected results. She said, "The experience . . . taught us not to hold preconceived ideas of what the neighborhood ought to have," but to discover "those things which the neighborhood would accept."

Another unexpected happening came to her in 1892 in the first years of Hull House and in the person of a total stranger. During a meeting, the speaker of the evening severely criticized the condition of a certain group of nearby buildings, tenements in the last stage of disrepair, squalor and dilapidation. He did not hesitate to mention the name of the owner who had let them fall into such condition and yet expected people to live in them.

The landlord thus criticized was William Kent. He was a young man, a resident of Chicago who was also accustomed to spend much of his time on a western ranch where wide horizons, freely blowing winds and long rides in the pleasant company of a mettlesome and obedient horse made up the order of his day. The crowded, dirty, rundown precincts of Chicago were far beyond his direct knowledge, even beyond his imagination. He had only lately inherited the property and had never seen it. When he heard of this denunciation in a place called Hull House, he registered high indignation — for a time.

Not long before, he had heard Jane Addams give a public address. Though she thought little of herself as a speaker, Jane was willing to spread the word anywhere about what Hull House was doing. She was singularly convincing, not by any emotional rhetoric, or any flights of oratory, but by her clarity and directness and her deep and unquestionable sincerity. Her subject had been "Shared Opportunities" and she had plainly pointed out the duty that well-to-do persons owed to the society that supported their prosperity. Like many other puzzled people, William Kent came now to Jane Addams for advice.

She said at once that they would go to look at the condition of the place in question. On the spot she spared him nothing, the derelict wooden tenements, the rickety outside stairs, the small, cracked windows, the leaking roofs, the filthy stables.

Standing in the midst of this desolation, well-clad, healthy, strong with good living, Kent was sickened at the thought that any place could be like this and that it belonged to him. Miss Addams called his attention to the tenants occupying certain of the dirtiest buildings, and told him that they were being used for disreputable purposes. "You might begin there," she suggested.

He did not relish what he saw, nor her advice when he received it. Like the "certain rich young man" of an earlier record, "he went away sorrowing."

In two weeks Jane saw William Kent again. He had been going over and over in his mind what he had seen, what she had suggested. "I have decided to turn over the property to you to use as you please," he declared.

He proposed to give her a free lease to the place and she was to use her own judgment about it. But, having a keen business eye, he warned her that if she tried to make the old houses habitable she would only be wasting her money. Even as it stood the place brought in two thousand dollars a year in rent.

It would make a public playground, she told him. There were none in Chicago, not even in connection with the schools. "The children have nothing but the streets now." Not for nothing had she said to her father so many years ago, "The children can come and play in my yard."

"You can do with it what you please," he returned. He was only anxious to have the possession of it off his conscience.

Would he pay for tearing down the buildings, she wished to know.

"I don't know why I should," he declared.

"And will you pay the taxes?" she went on.

"You ask too much," he replied abruptly and went away.

This time it was only a week before he came back. "I'll do whatever you say," he declared. They were friends henceforth, understanding each other and working together for the future. The playground was cleared, equipped and opened with a festival on May 1, 1892.

It had seemed somewhat inconsistent to discard an income of two thousand dollars a year when Hull House had no available funds even for setting the area up as a playground, but Jane agreed that Hull House would conduct and manage the place for ten years with William Kent carrying the taxes for five years more. It was found that three of the buildings could be sold and moved away. Chicago workmen made very little of moving buildings here and there. They were put up across the street with the agreement that they should not be used for a junkyard or a saloon.

In the midst of the inevitable protests of the tenants, most of them disreputable, who were to be dispossessed, the other derelict buildings were torn down. One old man told Jane, long after, that he had never again found a place "so like Italy." It was scarcely a tribute to his native land, but Miss Addams took it as it was meant to be understood.

The alderman of the ward saw to it that the playground and adjacent lots were flooded in cold weather for skating. The city government delegated a special policeman, George Murray, to keep order. He came to be a valued addition to the Hull House neighborhood. A stout, cheerful and friendly policeman can be an immense asset to the workers in any community effort.

In time a City Playground Commission was set up and offered to take over the responsibility of the playground along with the others that had been established elsewhere. Jane immediately agreed. One of her associates, Alice Hamilton, protested that public management would not be so efficient as the guidance of Hull House had been. But Jane insisted. Even if it were less well carried on, she believed, it would be something permanent. The children would have a place to play for all time, not just for the lifetime of Jane Addams or of Hull House.

VI

The Nineteenth Ward

The winter of 1893 after the close of the Columbian Exposition, that world's fair in which everyone took such pride, was a terrible one. Business fell off as in other depressions which have come in their extraordinary cycles but which society is only slowly learning to understand and to meet. Unemployment increased over the country. Conditions were worst of all in Chicago, where economic opportunity was already so unequal, where hordes of laboring men, attracted by the work of building and later tearing down the buildings of the fair, were now left with nothing to do. Banks were failing, factories closed their gates. The harsh winds blew in from Lake Michigan upon leaky tenements where there was no fuel. Men walked the streets rather than sit shivering at home where their children cried with hunger. Hull House had its hands full maintaining soup kitchens, offering what shelter and warmth it could manage, finding milk for starving babies as the needs mounted and mounted.

Jane Addams had with her at this time a truly wholehearted worker, Julia Lathrop. The two were hardly more than acquaintances when Julia first came to Hull House in 1890, but they already had much in common. Julia Lathrop had grown up in the town of Rockford, in a well-to-do family with much the same background as Jane's. Julia had been carefully educated according to a plan similar to that which John Addams had arranged for his daughter. And like Jane, Julia had felt within herself the capability of being of service to her fellow men and was eager to make use of it. Her father was a very successful lawyer; she also studied law but had no real taste for practicing it in that age when women lawyers were practically unknown. As has been said, she had attended Rockford Seminary for a year.

In one of her visits at home she had come over to the Seminary to help put on a scene of "the witches of *Macbeth*" which Rockford students were presenting and in which Jane was participating. Later when Jane and Ellen Starr were enlisting interest and support for Hull House, they spoke at Rockford, by that time Rockford College. Julia was immediately interested, for like William Kent she found Jane a moving and convincing speaker. Julia's father was not fully enthusiastic over his brilliant daughter's leaving home for the work and the place of living which she had chosen for herself. Yet he gave reluctant consent.

She had been appointed a county visitor in the city of Chicago, with her special district of inspection the region surrounding Hull House. It was natural that she would want to live there, among the first of those residents who were later to make up such a potent group. She was to become second only to Jane Addams as a strong supporting spirit in that great enterprise.

It was her duty to report to the city on the exact condition of the poor in the Hull House neighborhood. She found much suffering, and many cases where the county relief was overslow in coming and was administered with favoritism. There was but one center for distribution of food in the whole of Chicago and thither all must come from all over the city, standing for hours in long lines in the snow and rain, shepherded by policemen. "Burials are tardy and cruel" and conducted without any religious service at all. No wonder that of all things that the poor neighbors of Hull House dreaded, the chief thing was a pauper's grave.

So capable did Julia Lathrop prove as a county visitor that in 1892 she was appointed by Governor Altgeld to be a member of the state Board of Charities, a position of onerous duties, and like her first one, with no salary. It involved keeping records of all the state institutions, poorhouses, insane asylums, orphanages and hospitals. She was meticulous in carrying her responsibilities and singularly successful in achieving reforms. One of her friends from Hull House once accompanied her on an expedition of inspection of an abominably run institution for the insane and observed her method with its sulky and uncooperative superintendent.

He made bitter complaint of all the restrictions that were upon him and the scarcity of funds, thus giving excuse for every separate item of neglect and inefficiency. Julia Lathrop heard him out, each time offering ready sympathy, which finally won him a little from his defensive pose. When they returned to his office she firmly went over with him every single thing that was wrong, with wise suggestions about just how it was to be remedied. She pointed out to him, the friend said, "that after all he was the one in authority; if things were rotten it was he who must shoulder the responsibility," and she offered him no doubt at all as to how rotten she thought things were. "We left him evidently impressed and promising to do his best."

All the information which she gathered Julia Lathrop shared with Jane Addams and those who were working at Hull House. She was and always had been especially interested in the problems of youth. She reported that dependent children who had no one to support them were being housed in the county poorhouse in company with the old, the imbecile and sometimes even the insane. Teenagers who had been arrested for petty crimes and were being held for trial were kept in the common jail, in crowded filthy quarters, the girls in the company of vicious women, the boys with case-hardened criminals who were able instructors in the arts of breaking the law. Corruption in the city government made for a brutal and unjust police force, for overworked and careless petty magistrates and for unfair and hasty condemnations.

Julia had a delicate beauty, with her black hair and dark expressive eyes. She had also an unusually perceptive mind and a flashing wit. Although her work brought her into contact with perhaps the most miserable and depressing conditions and the ugliest scenes to be found in the big indifferent city, nonetheless she could always see a gleam of humor, a quirk of absurdity in the life which she was living. She was always carefully, although simply, dressed and carried with her an air of quiet elegance which did not put off the tired, blowsy women whom she visited, but inspired their wistful admiration. Some of these attributes might seem to belie the resolute character with which she pursued what Jane Addams called her "sense of moral obligation," a pursuit which she was to carry far.

Julia Lathrop

Although her daily work was absorbing and heavy, Julia Lathrop eagerly helped Jane Addams in the neighborly offices which she and Ellen Starr carried out. They were confronted one day with a duty which had not come their way before but which nonetheless did not daunt them. Word came by hasty messenger that a girl in a nearby tenement was having a baby and "was hollering something fierce; my mother says it's disgracing the whole house she is." None of the women who lived there would go to her with aid, for it had been decided among them that she was not respectable. And none of them would call a doctor for fear of being involved in paying him. The solution of the problem, like that of many others, was to call on the ladies of Hull House. Leaving someone to telephone for a doctor, Jane and Julia set out at once.

They found themselves, with no experience at all, plunged into the duty of assisting at the baby's birth — which they providentially managed with triumphant success — but alone, for the doctor did not get there until the baby was having his first bath and the mother was quiet and safe in a clean bed. They walked home, weary but relieved, through darkening streets in what Jane called the best moment of the day, when fathers were coming home from work, happily greeted by their children, and the mothers were comfortably preparing supper inside.

But for Jane the experience had been rather too much and she burst out, "This doing things we don't know how to do is going too far." She did not seem to fancy herself as a midwife.

Julia protested hotly against "beginning to hew down to our ignorance." To have refused to go to the help of the poor girl would have been a disgrace. If Hull House could not "have its roots in human kindness it is no good at all."

As the depression of the eighteen-nineties, which people then spoke of only as the Hard Times, moved on, it became steadily more evident that indiscriminate giving by personal and individual gifts was not making any impression upon the poverty which had grown so great under the errors of the too rapidly growing industrial system. Charity would have to be organized on a wider scale, must be based on a real knowledge of conditions, to be of any effect. And in a time like this, when the prosperity in which everyone had had such faith seemed to shrink away, the resources of private charity were a mere drop in the bucket in proportion to the vast need of a suffering population.

Only public assistance, only relief on a national scale with the resources of the federal government behind it could hope to make any perceptible impression. But this was not understood until much later, and Chicago struggled through its ordeal as best it might. Hull House had earlier given relief merely in a personal and neighborly way; its workers had been striving only to make better living conditions in the future; now they must occupy themselves with actual efforts to meet the emergencies of the moment. Yet the very intensity of the problems of the moment reemphasized the need for social changes later when circumstances would allow.

For Jane, Ellen Gates Starr and Julia Lathrop, life in this great city of Chicago was a voyage of discovery. They had all grown up in the atmosphere of the small country town, where everyone knew all about everyone else, a fact that in itself put a premium on honesty and integrity in public office. The first large truth that Jane Addams had discovered had been how good the poor were to one another.

The second was the extent and intricacy of corruption in city, county and state government.

Democracy has its vulnerable points, due to certain weaknesses in human nature. Democracy's toleration presents a situation in which, if enough of the voting citizens are sufficiently indifferent, and if even a small number are sufficiently unscrupulous, graft and dishonesty and misconduct of all kinds can creep in.

The city of Chicago was governed by a mayor and a council of aldermen made up of representatives of each ward. It is possible that Jane's father, who sat so long among the politicians of the Illinois legislature, knew of the state into which the city government of Chicago was falling, although we find no record of his ever having talked to his daughter of it. But no one could live long in Chicago, especially no one who was carrying on an enterprise for good, without discovering at every turn the unashamed misconduct existing in the state, county and city administrations.

The state institutions were a little better than those under county government, but in spite of that they had little to recommend them. In both cases the appointments of superintendents and civic officers were a matter of political patronage and were dealt out to those who were considered to have had earned favors in political campaigns. As a result, the heads of many state establishments for the blind, the insane, and orphan children were inefficient and totally indifferent to the welfare of those helpless ones so dependent upon them. The state Board of Charities which Julia Lathrop represented had no legal right to prosecute these administrators, no matter what were their shortcomings. Force of character could, however, do much and Julia

Lathrop left behind her a trail of astounded state appointees who had been shown their outrageous deficiencies with firm and quiet emphasis.

In the matter of Chicago's city government, country-bred Jane Addams had suffered a rude awakening. The council with its representatives from each ward had fallen into the hands of a group of grafters who ran the city's affairs in their own shamelessly dishonest fashion. People spoke of them as the "gray wolves."

The moneyed men of Chicago, the captains of industry, were too busy accumulating wealth in the competitive marketplace to pay much attention to what went on in city politics. Each financial leader well knew that city officials were fleecing him at every turn in the matters of building permits or streetcar and plumbing franchises, for which he always had to pay a premium to the alderman who procured them for him. Yet it was easier, quicker and cheaper in the end to suffer this than to exert political pressure for reform. Two of the aldermen in Chicago at this period have gone down in history for their grafting and avaricious ways. They were known familiarly as Hinky Dink Kenna and Bathhouse John Coughlin.

Kenna and Coughlin were the example to other and lesser actors in this large program of acquiring money and power while indifferent citizens looked on. Jane did not come in direct contact with these two local heroes. For her the whole scheme and method of city government, and the most direct obstacle to any change to more lawful methods, was represented in the large genial person of Johnny Power, prosperous saloon owner and alderman for the Nineteenth Ward, in which Hull House was situated. His district was nearly but not quite the most notorious in the city.

An alderman was elected to office by his ward. To be continually reelected, as John Power was, he had to remain in the good graces of his constituents. This he did by the affable benevolence which was one of his special gifts. He helped poor people who were in trouble over their rent or their delinquent children. No wonder that the woman who was so indignant when Miss Addams would not "speak to the judge" was so sure that her alderman could and would make things all right concerning her thefts. At Christmastime John, better known as Johnny Power, gave away literally tons of turkeys to his myriad friends. If one householder, by adroit management, should receive three or four stout carcasses, he could sell the surplus ones and no questions would be asked. Johnny Power attended christenings and weddings and was the life of the party. He was magnificent at funerals. He comforted bereaved and penniless relatives by insuring that their loved ones did not go to a pauper's grave.

Where did he get the funds for all this? The alderman's salary was small; it was only the beginning of his actual income, which came through an absolutely open and unblushing system of levying on those coming to seek his help who could afford to pay solidly for it. Opportunity to enlarge business premises, franchises for construction companies, commissions from the awarding of city contracts, and protection for gambling houses, all served his purpose. "Where did he get so much money?" the people asked. The satisfied answer of the Halstead Street neighbors was, "He gets it from the rich." They were not at all unwilling that the prosperous class should be despoiled for the sake of the poor. They blessed Johnny Power and "his big Irish heart" and would hear no wrong of him. A large number of those so busy redistributing Chicago's wealth to their own advantage were saloonkeepers and proprietors of gambling houses, like Hinky Dink, Bathhouse John, and Johnny Power.

The example of Hull House in starting clubs for boys to keep them out of mischief was followed here and there. One man from a neighboring church had organized a large group of boys whose principal object was to practice temperance in a saloon-ridden neighborhood. They were anxious to achieve the dignity of uniforms and this, as their leader so excitedly announced to Jane Addams one day, "the alderman" made possible by raising three thousand dollars from persons "with whom he was acquainted." It seemed ironic to Jane at first that an organization dedicated to temperance should be indebted for so large a favor to a man whose main business was a string of saloons and gambling houses. As she thought further, however, she realized what a disillusioning influence knowledge of this would have upon the ideas of the young boys who were concerned. She therefore set out with the help of the Hull House Men's Club to try to unseat this official who had been continuously reelected for twenty years.

Miss Addams was to learn in this early political experience by what well-established methods an alderman could guarantee his reelection. She had counted innocently on the neighbors' support of an honest attempt at political resistance to such blatant civic corruption. But she was not even yet fully acquainted with the nature and attitudes of the voters, those untutored immigrants who made up most of the citizenry of Ward Nineteen.

Johnny Power boasted that in one period of Hard Times he had got twenty-six hundred men of the ward put on the city payroll. Even after the stress was over, one man in five owed his job to the alderman. It was not easy to find very many who dared vote against him, for most were in fear of losing their jobs. Not even the leader of that boys' temperance brigade which had first aroused Jane's misgivings would campaign to unseat him, for there was that favor of three thousand dollars for which Power expected a return in loyalty.

A man complained to Jane that this year's votes sold for only two dollars apiece, instead of five in better times. Another man, a lodging-house keeper, sold all the votes in his house, taking a share of the returns that passed through his hands. Then he proceeded to sell them over again to the opposing party. This aroused furious indignation and brought outraged retaliation at the hands of the cheated purchasers of votes. They, or their party henchmen, seized the over-adroit financier and held him under an open street hydrant. His offense in the eyes of these agents of punishment was in reselling votes originally bought in so-called good faith, not in the least in his first transaction and original sale.

The Hull House forces rather easily succeeded in electing a member of their Men's Club to be the alderman colleague of John Power. But this person, alas, yielded to the temptations of the position, and was a dead loss to the campaign, becoming a willing disciple of Johnny Power. Undaunted, and under the spur of Jane Addams's steadfast intention, the Men's Club returned to the fray in the next election period. It was then found that every man who had been active in the first campaign had now been given a position by Johnny Power; a printer was now a clerk in the city hall; a teamster was in a well-paid place in the police stables; a bricklayer who had been the actual candidate running against Power was in the city building department. It was very difficult to find another candidate who would run. Each one who was asked insisted that he must have time to think the matter over, and each, during the interval, was bought off with political promises. Though a candidate, a young Italian, was at last found, he fell far short of being elected. Still Jane Addams and Hull House and its Men's Club persisted, and though Power was still elected in his third campaign, his majority was so reduced that the experience gave him food for thought. A certain improvement in the quality of his administration was evidence of this.

At this point, however, Jane Addams and her allies gave over. She could see now that John Power and his like impersonated the kind of political weed which flourished in the barren soil of the Nineteenth Ward which was not easily eradicated. It was one of her characteristics that she did not come to conclusions by sudden intuition or inclination; she studied an experience thoroughly and reasoned to a final opinion. It was of no use, she decided finally, to push through a reform "when the people were not ready for it." This was a belief that she was to apply in various crises later. But all Chicago had been watching the contest of wills between Hull House and civic corruption. The methods by which political chicanery held its own had been thoroughly exposed and would not so easily be followed thereafter.

It was evident that Alderman Power, on his part, plainly realized that he had had rather a narrow escape. He seemed to have no hard feelings. He said later, at the time when he had the playground flooded for skating, "I have the greatest

respect for Miss Addams and have had respect for her ever
since I have known her in her work in my ward. There has
never been any truce patched up between us, for the reason
that there has been no enmity. . . . If there are any favors
I could do for Hull House, and I have never been asked for
any, I would gladly perform them." The sinister note in this
statement was his assurance that any "favor" of any kind
would be possible for him to grant. But Jane Addams never
asked for one.

Although the feud between civic mismanagement and
the plans and purposes of Hull House did not persist there
were crying abuses and negligencies in the neighborhood
which could not be allowed to continue. The broken pave-
ments, the dirty. stables, of which there were countless
numbers in that horse-drawn age, the uncleaned alleys, all
witnessed the shocking negligence of the inspecting authorities. Against these conditions Jane Addams and Hull
House continued to make direct attacks.

The situation concerning garbage collection was the one
which cried out the most loudly for attention. In front of
every building a large wooden box was fastened to the
pavement. These receptacles for food and refuse of every
kind were grossly neglected by the politically appointed
contractor whose business it was to dispose of their contents.

Under pressure of complaints a little more was done to
improve matters, but it was perfectly plain that these great
bins were a bottomless source of evil odors, that children
played in them, eating any scraps that seemed remotely
edible and using other bits as missiles in their unending
games of cops and robbers. The Hull House Women's
Club, bravely pursuing a campaign during the hottest

months of the year further prepared a special report on the condition of alleys which literally stank to heaven.

Being unable to remove the alderman whose responsibility all this was, Jane, backed up by a group of businessmen, proceeded to put in a bid on her own account for the contract for the removal of the ward's garbage. The bid was thrown out on a technicality, but the matter caught the attention of the mayor and he appointed Jane official garbage inspector at a salary of a thousand dollars a year. It was the only paid office that she ever held.

One of her duties was to get up at six o'clock in the morning and follow the wagons to the city dump, to make sure that the refuse was actually collected and that not too much was spilled on the way. This she did faithfully in what the Hull House children came to call the "garbage phaeton," a somewhat deluxe model of the vehicle that pervaded America in the horse-and-buggy days. On one such expedition she took the mayor with her, that he might see for himself the nature and extent of her job.

At her insistence, the man who held the contract for garbage removal was forced to increase the number of his wagons from nine to nineteen. She brought careless landlords to book when they did not provide proper refuse receptacles. She saw that the filthy alleys were cleaned, and she made it emphatically clear that dirty rags, which the ragpickers carried home from the city dump to sort and wash in their own homes, were a fertile source of disease. Eventually she got a deputy to carry on the work for which she really had no time, and turned the salary over to her. But under her supervision the inspection continued to be so efficient that Johnny Power finally exerted his authority, got the position of garbage inspector abolished and the work turned over to a "ward superintendent" who, it was specified, must be a man. But a standard had been established which was not to be wholly disregarded. For years after, when Jane was asked to report to the current edition of *Who's Who* what official positions she had held, she always included the statement that she had been garbage inspector for Ward Nineteen.

After the flurry with Johnny Power was over, she managed on her own initiative to have the Chicago milk supply investigated by one of the professors of the University of Illinois. She laid his resulting report before the city authorities. The evidence of dirty milk was so undeniable that it could not be ignored, and the regulations were thereafter better enforced. The death rate for Ward Nineteen, especially among babies in summer, had been the third highest in the city; it dropped to seventh, thanks to the intervention of Hull House.

The people of Chicago and the public press were beginning to take note of what Jane Addams and Hull House were accomplishing. Her name was respected and praised everywhere; she was spoken of as one of the foremost citizens of Chicago. She was probably by far the most popular, for a time.

But things can suddenly and inexplicably change. Jane's tilt with Johnny Power was, it turned out, only a small skirmish. The real battle was to come. She was to lose all her justly earned popularity; she was to be mercilessly criticized and decried by the newspapers.

VII

Haymarket Square

The cause of Jane Addams's emerging unpopularity, which reached in time such staggering proportions, was after all not far to seek. The immediate and evident success of her work at Hull House had made her a definitely prominent woman in the eyes of the public and the press. Distinguished leaders and thinkers in Chicago were allying themselves with what was going on at Hull House. She herself was an able speaker and was beginning to be invited in all directions when there were occasions for making an address. Although at first Jane and Ellen Starr attempted to carry Hull House expenses on their own slender incomes, it was very early evident that its rapid growth was getting far beyond their means.

In 1894 they therefore decided, with some reluctance, that they must be incorporated and must set up a board of trustees. Accordingly, a group of devoted men and women became trustees of Hull House. They lent advice and generous material aid. In the articles of incorporation, when Hull House Associates were chartered, the summary of their efforts was stated, among other things, to be "to investigate and improve the conditions in the industrial districts of Chicago."

At first the subject of most of Jane's speeches was the nature of a social settlement in itself and where it could hope to give help to the neighborhood round about it. But as time went on, she stressed more and more the object of investigation, looking toward much needed improvements. She herself became more aware of the real state of affairs in the rapidly growing industrial quarters of the city. She saw that conditions of labor were not only deplorable but were rapidly growing worse. Low wages, cruelly long hours, bad working conditions of foul air and dangerous, unguarded machinery, were considered by employers to be an unavoidable part of the competitive system. Manufacturing expenses must be kept down to the lowest possible level that labor would or could endure.

Labor's single defense against such conditions rested in the trade unions. Their only active weapon when they were pushed beyond protest was the strike. In an earlier period, trade unions had been outlawed and classed as illegal conspiracies, but this attitude had given place to a more enlightened one, so they were now forming on all sides. They had no very great number of members, their funds were very small, and being inexperienced in the essential art of collective bargaining, they made their own mistakes, just as they do now that they are huge and immensely rich.

The attitude of the employers, for the most part, was pure resentment. Each tried to keep the unions out of his particular company as long as possible. Their only idea of what to do about a strike was to break it, even if it called for the use of force. The supply of labor was overplentiful, so non-union men could always be found to take the places of the strikers who were discharged from their jobs on the spot. The employers were organized too, more effectively even than the workers. The enmity between the two sides made for greater and greater pressure.

Such conditions were growing up in industry all over the country but they were palpably worse in Chicago. To understand something of the tension and what followed, it is necessary to go back to that harsh and bitter moment in Chicago's history, which everyone remembered but of which people spoke little, the time of the Haymarket Riot of May 4, 1886. The ranks of Chicago workingmen of that time contained a good many socialists and a small number of anarchists. Socialists, in that day, stood for government or municipal ownership and operation of all principal businesses. This prospect, coupled with the corruption of the Chicago city government, did not offer much to tempt clear-thinking persons, let alone businessmen. The anarchists were a far less numerous body, most of them Russians who had fled pogroms and oppression in their own country. They differed from the socialists by insisting that if reform could not be achieved by peaceable methods, then it was obligatory to use violence. In a succession of strikes that took place in the spring of 1886, the demands were for an eight-hour day with the same pay as the longer one. This seemed to many employers preposterous and certainly impossible.

When a strike for shorter hours occurred at the Mc-Cormick reaper works, the company turned off its whole force of seasoned employees and reopened with nonunion men. On Monday, May 3, 1886, at the close of work, a fight took place at the gates of the McCormick plant

[97]

between the strikebreakers and the union pickets walking outside. A large crowd gathered. The police were summoned and were ordered to fire into the crowd, which they did, killing two union men and wounding many others. A meeting of protest was called for the next evening, May 4, to be held at Haymarket Square, located at the widening of the street space at Randolph, on the West Side.

The meeting was not a very large one, not much over a thousand people, and in spite of some inflammatory speeches, remained a quiet one. Large numbers of police had been alerted but there seemed to be little need for them. The current mayor, Carter Harrison, had come to look on, but told the chief of police that it was an orderly crowd and there would be no trouble. It began to rain. A man named Fielding was addressing the crowd. An officious person ran to the police to report that he was using dangerous language and the police began to move in.

The crowd had dwindled to about two hundred. Fielding was just winding up his speech. "In conclusion . . ." he was saying, when a missile with a lighted fuse cut through the air, hissing in the rain. It dropped before the front line of the approaching police and went off with a deafening explosion. Seven policemen were fatally injured, a large number wounded. Their commanding officer ordered them to fire, which they did. Spectators were hit and wounded, two of the speakers among them. Sixty-seven policemen had been hurt, some by the bomb itself, others by police bullets. No one ever knew who threw the bomb.

Panic raced through Chicago as it had through Washington the night Lincoln was assassinated. Avowed anarchists had been among the speakers at the meeting. It was plain, so everyone believed, that here was an anarchist plot to seize the city government, to put an end to law and order, to deprive citizens of their property, even of their lives! There had been recent revolutionary uprisings in Paris. Here, men told one another, was more of the same thing. Even when unreasoning terror had somewhat died down, there was a loud call for the complete destruction of the anarchist group.

Police went everywhere, searched houses, confiscated papers, brought accusations. Finally, since no single person could be found guilty, a whole group of men were indicted as accessories to the murder of Matthias Dugan, one of the policemen who had been killed. Trial opened with seven prisoners in the dock. One of those accused, Albert Parsons, could not be found or arrested but in the course of the first day's proceedings he appeared and gave himself up to be tried with the others. Since there was no evidence that any one of them had thrown the bomb, it seemed as though in justice they would all be acquitted. But the court did not intend that they should escape.

The newspapers and loud voices from the still-alarmed public demanded that somebody, almost anybody it seemed, must be hanged. Two young lawyers of the Central Labor Union took the task of defending the accused men, assisted by a more experienced attorney, Captain William Black, who was immediately accused of being an anarchist himself. He attempted to get the case put before Judge Tuley, of whom Jane Addams had occasion to think highly. Tuley could have been trusted to grant a fair trial, but that was not what the public wanted. The case was brought before Judge Joseph Gary.

When a jury is being chosen, it is the law that if a proposed juryman has already made up his mind about the guilt of the person or persons under trial, he must be rejected. This law Judge Gary openly flouted. He appointed Henry Ryce a special bailiff to receive and select the proposed jurymen. Ryce declared, voicing the open policy of the court, "Those fellows are going to hang as sure as death." Man after man, summoned for jury duty, admitted that he had already determined that the accused were guilty and deserved death. The defense lawyers were allowed only a certain number of challenges; when these were exhausted, jurymen were accepted entirely as Henry Ryce chose. The trial opened with almost the whole jury already committed to a conviction. Not one of the jurors finally chosen represented labor.

The state's attorney acted on the assumption that there was "a gigantic conspiracy" to destroy all government; all the anarchist leaders who approved it were guilty of the crime. No witness appeared who could give convincing evidence about who threw the bomb. But the court did not feel the need of evidence; it was looking only for conviction. In his instructions to the jury, Judge Gary declared that it was not necessary to know the identity of the bomb thrower. One of the eight men tried who had only the smallest imaginable connection with the events on May 4 was given fifteen years in prison. The other seven, including Albert Parsons, who had given himself up, were condemned to death.

Although not one newspaper in the country undertook to criticize Judge Gary's conduct of the trial, there were many in Chicago who were not satisfied that justice had been done. An Amnesty Association was organized to try for a pardon or to get the sentences commuted to life imprisonment, both of which were within the power of the governor of Illinois. Judge Gary had refused to allow a new trial. The Supreme Court of Illinois upheld Gary's decision and declared that the trial had been fair. The United States Supreme Court decided that it had no jurisdiction in a case of this special kind.

In the Amnesty Association was Henry Demarest Lloyd, a friend and ardent supporter of Jane Addams and a trustee of Hull House. He with others waited on the governor in Springfield and got from him a statement that he would commute the sentences to life imprisonment if the men would forswear their anarchistic views. Two of the eight men agreed and asked for mercy. Their sentences were commuted but the rest would not recant.

Feelings ran high all over the country and even abroad. There was a mass meeting in London, addressed by important leaders, protesting the conduct of the Chicago judge and the unfairness of the trial. On the day before the execution, one of the remaining five prisoners committed suicide in the jail. The four who were left were hanged. One wonders, what, on that day, were the feelings of the person who actually threw the bomb.

Many years later, when this writer was a little girl living in a town at a distance from Chicago, she heard one of her teachers say on a dark November morning, "It was a day like this when the anarchists were hanged."

The memory and self-questioning of that occasion went very deep, even with those who were far outside the immediate scene. But the three men who had been spared disappeared into the state prison; the anarchy scare died down and the years began to go by. Each new governor was asked to release the surviving prisoners, but to no avail.

All this had come to pass two years before Hull House

was opened, but the events of that tragic time affected Jane Addams nonetheless. The Haymarket Riot and its consequences naturally widened the breach between employers and working people, and Jane Addams was to see them growing farther and farther apart. Chicago was by no means a wicked assemblage of cruel persons, exploiting those who toiled for them and building fortunes on their labor. The city was full of hundreds and thousands of honest, good-hearted people doing their best to carry on their lives and care for their families in a decent society. But those whom Jane Addams called the "Captains of Industry" had evolved the policy of depressing wages and skimping expense on working conditions, in the false idea that this was the only way to make a profit. Jane could see the pressures and problems of both sides, but the recurring question, what can be done about it, was not easily answered, since the confusion and blackness of the whole situation was yet to be fully understood.

Miss Addams said several times that she thought of Hull House as a bridge between the prosperous and the less prosperous, the happily secure and those who could not be certain of an adequate living for themselves or their own. She felt to cross that bridge was good for all, that those who gave were as blessed and awakened as those in need who received. There were some who were able to cross it and some who were not.

An early friend of Hull House was George Pullman, founder and president of the Pullman Palace Car Company. He was interested, as far as he saw it, in the welfare of his employees, who as the company prospered came to be numbered in hundreds and presently in the thousands. He built the thriving little town of Pullman south of

Chicago, with neat brick houses for the employees to rent, or even to buy, with clean streets and parks and fountains. Anyone passing by it on the train could not fail to be struck by its shaven lawns, its trees, its schools and churches, its arcade of stores, the forerunner of the modern shopping center. Such well-keeping was firmly required of the Pullman workers. They must also live in Pullman houses and buy at Pullman stores. George Pullman looked forward to the time when the place would be known all over the world as the pattern of what an industrial town should be.

Disaster came when business began to slacken. The number of workers was greatly reduced and so were wages, without any reduction in rents, in rates for gas and water, in prices in the stores. Repeated protests to Mr. Pullman proved unavailing and in May of 1893 the men struck. The dispute did not look like a difficult one to settle, but George Pullman made it impossible.

Outsiders offered to mediate and a Citizens' Arbitration Committee was formed, of which Jane Addams was invited to be a member. She was asked to be the committee's representative at the first meeting that the strikers held in a town near Pullman. There she listened attentively as the workers stated their wrongs and their needs. In spite of her friendship with George Pullman, her sympathies went out entirely to his workingmen.

But no effort at negotiation or persuasion could move Mr. Pullman. A man, he maintained, had a right to run his business as he saw fit. When he was asked whether he would submit to the men's pleas for arbitration he only responded, "There is nothing to arbitrate."

His men stood just as stoutly by their position and the strike dragged on with growing ill-feeling and hardship, and finally with increasing violence. The American Railway Union went out on strike against the Pullman Company in sympathetic protest, and George Pullman appealed to President Cleveland for federal troops to protect his property. The governor of Illinois, John Altgeld, had declared that the state militia was all that was needed to keep order, but George Pullman and President Cleveland insisted on federal aid. Pullman insisted also until the bitter end that "there is nothing to arbitrate." The federal troops broke the strike which had dragged through weary months until the men and their families were nearly starving.

The depth of feeling aroused by this strike was evidenced three years later when there came to see Miss Addams a man who had been one of George Pullman's superior workers, an Englishman of great skill and respectability. He had found it almost impossible to get employment after being discharged from the Pullman Company on account of the strike. At last, under an assumed name, he had found a place in the repair shop of a streetcar company. But the truth of his having been a leader in the Pullman trouble had come to light and he had been summarily discharged again. As Jane Addams said, "He seemed to me to be the epitome of the wretched human waste such a strike implies."

The whole struggle had only caused the chasm between labor and management to widen again with mutual suspicion and ill-feeling. Hatred that is born of fear is deep and lasting, and trouble arises from it again and again. The main struggle at this time was over the eight-hour day, but it seemed as though it would have to be dropped as a goal hopeless to achieve. In this situation it began to be more and more evident that Jane Addams, in her actions and her public speeches, was showing how steadily she and Hull House stood on the side of the trade unions.

Jane took no further part in the Pullman affair beyond attending that one meeting of the men who were on strike. Her beloved older sister, Mary Addams Linn, fell desperately ill and died about that time, leaving her youngest son to Jane's guardianship. Yet for that one occasion of her hearkening to the complaints of the men, George Pullman never forgave her. He withdrew his yearly and once generous subscriptions to Hull House. He died not many years after, one of those who could not cross Jane's bridge between his world and that of his workmen. That was his tragedy — and theirs.

The Pullman Company went on under other management, that of Robert Lincoln, the only one of the great President's children who survived him. A court had decided that an employer had no legal right to dictate the conditions of living for his workers. Under the new administration parks were abandoned, the fountains were shut off, the smooth lawns allowed to grow ragged. The model town was a model no longer, if in truth it ever had been one.

The public press was scarcely better than George Pullman in its prejudice against Miss Addams as a "dangerous liberal" because of her support for trade unions. Although Jane could see the weaknesses of the unions and how much they had to learn, she steadfastly believed that the unions would in time break down the blind principle that ownership could permanently override the rights of labor. She saw unions exposed to corruption and inner dissension, but she was sure that they could learn to resist them. She deplored the use of the strike as the inevitable weapon, having seen its grinding hardships, its savage violence and the unforgiving bitterness it left in its wake. Yet she stood by the unions. As a result there began to be little limit to the abuse that was heaped upon her. The young nephew, for whom she was guardian and who later wrote her biography, could recall of his own knowledge that some people were saying "she should be hanged on the nearest lamppost."

Very early there had been formed at Hull House a Working People's Social Science Club. It met weekly with an invited speaker followed by discussion and questions. Any person who wished to advance his theories was given a hearing, socialist, anarchist or whatever he was. The presence of this club and the freedom of speech which it allowed was judged by many to be a threat to society. Actually, since all sorts of beliefs could be aired and argued, it gave an outlet to pent-up feelings and opinions. But the excited scenes that sometimes developed at the meetings brought some undue prominence to Hull House and to Jane. Nevertheless she steadily refused to have the Working People's Club removed; she was certain that its function was a salutary one.

Later, the Averbuch incident was another occasion for hostile publicity. A young Russian, newly come to Chicago and unable to find work, went to see the chief of police, on what special errand no one ever knew. That official, at sight of a stranger who addressed him in broken English, instantly concluded that here was an anarchist come to assassinate him. He called loudly for help, drew his pistol and emptied it into the boy's body, killing him instantly. It was proved that Averbuch was an anarchist, but he was totally unarmed and whatever his errand, it seems to have been quite innocent. There was great furor over the matter in the newspapers, but only on the basis of its being further proof of "an anarchist plot."

The police had sought out Averbuch's sister, and tried, by giving her the third degree of questioning, to get her to own to the so-called plot. A group of the Averbuchs' compatriots came to Jane in great distress over the tragedy that had overwhelmed both brother and sister. She undertook to have the affair investigated and the police brought to book for their treatment of Olga Averbuch. It was difficult to find a lawyer who would undertake such a case, but at last she came upon a young man of liberal views, Harold Ickes by name, who assumed the responsibility of establishing the truth. Jane felt that his doing so at least could reassure the terrified immigrants that justice and fairness were still available in their new country.

Nobody could ever really question that Jane Addams was completely fair-minded in seeing each side of the labor disputes which she was so often asked to mediate. She did not hesitate to allow strike meetings to be held at Hull House, and various women's trade unions were first discussed and organized there. A very large proportion of the women in industry were young girls of the very age in which she was so much interested, who had no knowledge of how to bargain with employers. It was under the direct auspices of Hull House that unions of women shirtmakers and cloakmakers were organized.

In certain quarters Jane's reputation grew steadily. She was asked again and again to help mediate in labor disputes, for the working people had unshakable trust in her. She was appointed to many arbitration boards when a law requiring arbitration was passed by the legislature. It was, however, one of the characteristics of Illinois laws of that time that they were often unenforced. The real nature of her stand in the midst of this period of labor quarrels and difficult settlements was once forcefully stated by herself.

She had been addressing an outdoor meeting and a heckler in the crowd on the sidewalk shouted at her, "You won't talk like this when the millionaires begin to subsidize you!"

Her answer was immediate, "I don't intend either to be subsidized by millionaires, or bullied by labor-unionists. I expect to keep on saying what I think without consulting either of them." To her relief and reassurance, her audience broke into delighted applause.

Her unusual capacity for sympathetic and intelligent understanding gave her special advantage in the study of labor disputes and in her conviction that collective bargaining was far better means of settlement than the strike. She was a just friend of the employers as well as of the laborers, but it was labor that understood and appreciated her long before the others did. She was to increase in wisdom and skill in the analysis of these difficult situations and in her ability to suggest the possible ways out. A most significant instance of what she was able to accomplish came several years after the Pullman strikes, but the incident may well be recounted here along with her other connections with the trade unions.

A very large clothing company, Hart, Schaffner and Marx, employing a great number of young women, had difficulty over wages. It began with a foreman's cutting the wages of a sixteen-year-old girl by a quarter of a cent per garment. She "walked out," though without any idea of its being a union matter. Other girls followed her until the whole huge Hart, Schaffner and Marx organization was idle. The main workrooms and shops were pleasant enough, but various smaller places connected with the company were not much better than sweatshops. It was an enormous strike and commanded public attention everywhere.

Jane Addams was one of an arbitration committee of three who were to pass final judgment on proposals offered by the two sides. When one plan was drawn up and submitted, Jane objected to it. The employers had passed on the union's proposal, but when it was submitted to the arbitration board, a clause forbidding collective bargaining had been added. Jane returned the agreement to the leaders of the union side, saying that their members never would or should accept it.

The union representative had already signed it, saying that in his opinion it contained as much concession from the employers as they could hope to get. But in spite of persuasion, Miss Addams refused to sign it as arbitrator, and negotiations had to be reopened. They dragged on for months but Jane would not give way. She insisted that without collective bargaining there could be no permanent way of settling future disputes, which were bound to arise again and again. The strike lasted from September to January. Finally a collective bargaining agreement was achieved which was satisfactory to both sides. It was accepted and signed. The result gave Hart, Schaffner and Marx the distinction of being the leaders in adjusted labor relations. Jane had stood out against Harry Hart, president of the company, and Sidney Hillman, head of the garment workers' union and formerly a Hull House resident. Both men realized the strength of her courage and justice and remained her friends always.

VIII

A Factory Law

After the Hard Times, Chicago became once more a highly prosperous city, second only to New York in numbers and activities, with a far larger rate of growth. Such rapid expansion of size and of business enterprise necessarily left behind many evils unremedied. Canon Barnett, Jane's old friend in London, the founder of Toynbee Hall, passed through Chicago on a journey round the world, and came to see her and Hull House. Even after the slums of London, he found conditions in Chicago shocking.

He did not realize how different the problems were from those which Toynbee Hall had to meet, for here were the countless newly arrived immigrants, many from rural districts at home, whose traditional habits of living had to be reconsidered and adapted to the necessities of a huge, crowded city. He was shocked to see that the Greeks were allowed to slaughter sheep in the basements of the houses near Halstead Street, that bakers produced bread in filthy cellars under the street and purveyed it to the households round about. Jane Addams had already learned what a long time and effort were needed to accomplish the drastic changes that were necessary in this situation, when Chicago was justly called "a mosaic of foreign cities." She was willing to be patient and she began to realize that the labor of accomplishing the necessary reform might well reach beyond her time.

Meanwhile Hull House, like Chicago, was growing lustily. Both were young, experimental, and faced with abounding opportunities. And it must be remembered that a goodly measure of Chicago's people were generous and openhearted, and a sufficient number of them, through thick and thin, supported Jane and her group of workers on Halstead Street.

By now, a striking and effective figure had been added to their number. Early on a bitterly cold morning, just before New Year's Day of 1892, there appeared on the doorstep of Hull House Mrs. Florence Kelley and her three children. They were not alone as they waited after ringing the bell, for with them was a tall, dark, silent person, a Kickapoo Indian, Henry Standing Bear, also asking for admittance. Miss Addams herself opened the door. On one arm she had a fat baby that belonged to the cook and with the other hand she was leading a prancing little Italian girl whose mother had left her there while she went to fetch a bundle of clothing from the sweatshop, to be finished at home. The little girl was anxious to run out into the windy cold, but Jane managed to restrain her and to shut the door against the cutting blast that swept in from the lake.

"We were greeted as though we had been invited," Florence Kelley said afterward, telling how they had all come in and were welcomed and warmed and substantially fed. Standing Bear stated his need for work, which was easily met by giving him temporary employment in the heating department. But Florence Kelley's problem was more complicated.

She was of Quaker parentage, as she explained to Miss Addams, and had been brought up in Philadelphia. She had studied at Cornell, then one of the few colleges offering higher education to women. In a class on Swinburne she had met a young Quaker girl from Baltimore, Martha Carey Thomas.

After Florence Kelley graduated from Cornell she wished to achieve a higher degree abroad. She went to Heidelberg, was admitted for study but was refused the privilege of applying for a degree. Nor did it seem that she could hope for one from any other European university. It happened, however, that at Avignon she came once more upon Carey Thomas, who was one day to become president of Bryn Mawr College. Miss Thomas told of her having been granted a Ph.D. degree in Switzerland at the University of Zurich. She suggested that Florence Kelley apply there and gave her directions for how it was best done. Florence followed her advice, and was graduated from Zurich.

Florence Kelley had traveled much with her father, who was interested as she was in industrial conditions, particularly those applying to working children. In America he had taken her to inspect a steel mill where she had seen little boys working in the withering heat and glow of the great dippers with their huge and dangerous loads of molten steel. It was the boys' duty to bring buckets of water to the ever-thirsty men. In England the Kelleys toured the Midlands, the Black Country of mines and factories, and had a chance to see the women working at home making nails and chains.

One poor woman, with tears rolling down her cheeks, told them her pitiful story of desperate poverty while hammering away at the links of the chain that she was forging, unable to take the time to stop even for a moment of talk. In cases of rush orders there was absolutely no account of extra time, even when it extended far into the night. Work was so difficult to find that there were a dozen women waiting to seize her place once she felt driven to give it up.

During her study in Switzerland Florence Kelley met and fell in love with a young Polish-Russian doctor. She was married to him in 1884. His work was not very successful in Europe so they came to New York, where the second and third of their children were born. Her husband was unable to set up a practice there, either, so finally, in desperation, she divorced him, getting custody of the children and permission to use her maiden name. She was "an avowed socialist" but managed to be expelled from the party, possibly for insubordination, although she said her fellow socialists were suspicious of her because she spoke English so fluently. She had dedicated herself to work toward mitigating the hardships of working women and working children. Hearing in New York of Hull House, she had come without any previous arrangement in the hope of working there.

Jane took her measure at once and acted promptly and effectively, as she always knew how to do. She took the travelers in for the night and the next day went with them to Winnetka to see Mr. and Mrs. Henry Demarest Lloyd, Jane's friends in many projects. Mrs. Lloyd readily agreed to take in the children, who in Winnetka would be within visiting reach of their mother and could not have been better placed. Florence Kelley was offered the position at Hull House of vocational advisor to young working girls. In her small room that overlooked the Hull House court and its little fountain, she settled down to residence and to an extremely vigorous and happy career.

Hers was an absolutely indomitable spirit. It has been said that her method of attaining her ends was "by direct assault." She was unsparing in her efforts and immensely effective at any work to which she put her hand. In looking into opportunities for the girls she was advising, she came on conditions which she considered intolerable, and complained to the state board of labor. This body had advisory functions but no executive power. Yet after her prolonged efforts they at last authorized her to make an official survey of working conditions in the area in which Hull House stood, a task to which she set herself with ability and enthusiasm. Julia Lathrop was already reporting on living conditions there. Enough of these reports eventually reached the state legislature to influence the establishment of a commission to look further into the matter of industrial affairs in Chicago. Florence Kelley conducted the members of the commission on an inspection tour and did not spare them the sight of a typical sweatshop in full operation.

The sweatshops of New York and Chicago in those years of the 1890s were real abominations, which it seems incredible now that society allowed to endure. Not a great many people knew, perhaps, how bad they were, and a great many preferred not to know. "Tenement work" was allowed with very little attempt at regulation. Such licensing as was supposedly required was complacently violated, un-

Florence Kelley

enforced and actually unenforceable. The "sweaters" were small-caliber agents, mostly in the garment trades, who received work prepared by the cutters in a central factory and parceled it out to their employees working at home, saving the sweaters the expense of rent or fuel or proper workshop equipment.

These small employers did not even undertake the fetching and carrying involved; men and, more frequently, women could be seen every day staggering under great bundles of unfinished clothing, carried out to be completed at home. Practically all the ready-made clothes sold in department stores and even a great deal of those specially made to order were manufactured in this way. In the very finest stores the most expensive garments were thus prepared for the market. Mrs. Smythe-Jones-Robinson might go to the opera in a cloak which only a day or two before had come out of some tenement dwelling where dirt, vermin and germs of every sort of disease reigned unchecked. It was the duty of an official inspector — although that duty was not specified in official language — to make sure that none of the vermin that a garment inevitably carried away with it would get so far as the salesrooms. The germs, being less conspicuous, were left undisturbed.

Florence Kelley made certain that the commission saw everything. No one could look upon those nightmare scenes and fail to realize that here was an evil which must be eradicated. Mrs. Kelley's reports were straightforward and factual, they gave the plain details but they did not quite convey the whole situation.

What a sweatshop was really like can be learned from the picture drawn by young Walter Wyckoff, who was preparing himself for a career in teaching social subjects at

Princeton. Wycoff felt that to understand fully what a working man faced in America he must try, at least briefly, to be a working man himself. He has given account of how he set out, with no money, to make his way — on foot — from the eastern seaboard across the country to California, earning his living by the way. He spent the winter of 1891–1892 in Chicago, where even before the Hard Times had actually begun, and while the World's Fair was still being built, thousands of men were unemployed. Not even a skilled laborer could find work, unless he put his hand to the meanest and most temporary job. When he was briefly in funds, though never more than by a few dollars, Wyckoff would pass the nights in a laboring man's flophouse; when he was penniless he slept on the floor of the police station. He made an effort, besides the great one of keeping himself from the edge of starvation, to see the sights of Chicago which had bearing on the work he was preparing himself to do. He saw sweatshops in various places and vividly describes an entirely typical, entirely horrifying one.

The small room that he depicts is crowded to suffocation, men, women and children crammed together among the rows of sewing machines, for this is where the family lives, sleeps and cooks meals as well as works. Very small children crawl on the floor among the machines, slightly larger ones of three and four sit on stools at their mothers' feet, also at work. Besides the men and women there are boys and girls of ten, twelve, fourteen or sixteen, all sitting at the heavy, noisy, foot-power machines, their backs bent, their eyes fixed immovably on their work. In a corner of the room is an alcove with a gasoline or charcoal stove, where the garments are pressed. The machines are run at the highest possible speed, for not a minute can be wasted of the ill-paid hours of the working day if they are to cover the meanest possible version of living. The noise is deafening.

High against the wall is a clothesline where hang the finished and gloriously handsome garments that will presently go forth for sale to the wives and daughters of Chicago's millionaires. Do any of the women look up at them with covetous eyes, picturing themselves possessed of such richness? Not one; they cannot stop to think of anything other than the task before them. The unfinished garments go from hand to hand, each person doing a small part of the assembling and finishing. The workers are paid by the piece, ten cents for sewing on a gross of buttons; seams and buttonholes paid in proportion. The last to work on them are the children, pulling out the basting threads before the garment goes to the presser in the corner. Children of that age are paid four and a half cents an hour, slightly older ones a little more, so that by ten hours' work they can earn from forty-five to sixty cents a day.

The workroom is usually in a basement or at the top of a rickety and crowded wooden staircase; there is no water supply but the hydrant in the courtyard. The place, with its charcoal stove, is a firetrap beyond imagining. A policeman comes in to make an inspection, but no busy worker takes time to look up at him. He makes brief note of the foul air and the dirty floor, and as he is going out, observes a heap of garbage spilled in a corner.

This is too much. "You've got to clean up here, right away," he says. "The first thing you know you'll start a fever that will sweep the city before we can stop it."

Someone does finally pay attention to him. A young Russian, hardly more than a boy, working at the machine nearest to the door, turns to answer. "What time do we have to keep clean when it's all we can do to get bread?" he shouts above the thunder of the machines. "Don't talk to us about disease, it's bread we're after, bread!"

Jane Addams learned a great deal in those arbitration sessions between laborers and employers. She became familiar with many details of working conditions which even her visits among the neighbors had not revealed to her before. She learned of further evils through studying the reports brought in by Julia Lathrop and Florence Kelley. It was always her practice to take no important step before full information was collected and appraised as the basis for final decision.

A settlement, she maintained, was in a specially favored position to gather such information and recommend the use of it. She began to feel that it was time for some drastic measure, so she and her colleagues set about working for what was to be the first real factory law for the state of Illinois.

Now began not just a battle but a long and relentless war, a crusade against the overwhelming poverty and unjust working conditions which the rapid advance of industry had unthinkingly brought about.

By 1893 Jane and her Hull House associates had, with hard work, succeeded in making the individual lives of their poor neighbors more bearable. The big rooms were filled with activity, with clubs and classes of every kind, crowded classes in English, classes in wood- and metal-working for the boys, in sewing and cooking for the girls, in art and in music. There was a Shakespeare club, a dramatic club, and dozens of others. No demand or need showed itself for which effort had not been made to find an answer. Corresponding to the Jane Club, the organization for cooperative living by working girls, there was now the Phalanx Club for young men.

Some old men in the neighborhood who liked to read philosophy and argue over it had asked for a Plato Club, which Julia Lathrop conducted with skill and clarity, humor and understanding. One old man always made it his business to differ from her in any philosophical discussion that arose. At one point, when he accidently happened to align himself on the same side with her, she commented on the fact that he had at last agreed with her. "I agree with you, Miss Lathrop? Not at all," he returned. "It is you who agree with me!" The club was much amused over this, especially when Julia Lathrop replied that either he, she or Plato must have shifted in opinion, and that she was sure it was not Plato.

A young professor of philosophy at the nearby University of Chicago, named John Dewey, used to address the Plato Club from time to time. He was to become a leader in the philosophy of the education of children and was a staunch friend of progress.

Jane Addams's interest in young people continued to be untiring. She raised her voice, perhaps the only voice heard at that time, for improvement in the lives and work of young girls in domestic service, of which there were thousands in the households of prospering Chicago. The word servant is almost obsolete in our society today and well it may be. The artificial subservience which a household worker was supposed to maintain before an employer, and the complete dependence on that employer's whim or convenience, was then unquestioned. The long hours of work, the brief and often uncertain intervals of time off, the absence of paid vacations, were all equally unjust.

But what Jane stressed most was the utter loneliness of such a life. Cut off for most of the week from any association with home and family, completely separated from the household in which she was employed, a girl spent solitary evenings in those houses where she was the only worker. All these, Jane felt, were peculiar and unnecessary hardships. Such girls were encouraged and welcomed at Hull House; their employers were reassured as to their spending their free time there and were urged to be more generous with it. At Hull House there was opportunity for girls to form friends, both with other girls and with young men, a chance at last to live a more normal life.

Ever since that first Christmas party when the little girls could not look at candy because they had been working for sixteen hours a day in the factory that made it, Jane had been relentlessly set against child labor in all its ugly forms. Not even the fiery Florence Kelley was more irreconcilably determined that it must come to an end.

The legal age for a child to receive a license to leave school and go to work was fourteen, although it was a ruling more honored in the breach than in the fulfillment. The enemies of the system were not only the employers looking for cheap labor, but also the parents who, some with a profound sense of thrift, some out of mere greed, would put their children out to work as soon as they could plausibly do so. They had to sign an affidavit that the child was of legal age for working, but it was easy to sign affidavits which never seemed to be questioned — until Florence Kelley appeared on the scene.

Parents, as Jane was constantly reminded, were required to sign a release exonerating the employer from responsibility in the case of accidents to child workers. The child was required to carry in his pocket a card of warning, put in extremely adult language, concerning the machinery in the midst of which he toiled, giving directions against getting too close to the wheels or against touching the spinning belts when they were in motion. For children who scarcely spoke English and who had not been in school long enough to learn to read, this was little protection.

One of the most hideous abuses which Florence Kelley brought to light was a practice mainly found in the glass factories at Alton, Illinois, but which was not unknown elsewhere. Certain labor agents, going about to the poorhouses and asylums of the state, would seek out the dependent children who had no parents, or had been abandoned by them, and would get themselves made legal "guardians." They would then bring their wards to work in the fearful heat of the glass factory, carrying away finished bottles and bringing molds and new material. The glassblower, who was a highly skilled workman, depended for the full pay for his piecework on the rapidity of his small helper, and kept him trotting back and forth at the highest possible speed. At the end of the day the boy would duly trot after the man whose "dog" he was, to seek the refreshment that complete exhaustion called for in the nearest saloon. The guardians of these wretched children lived on their pitiful wages. Those ten years old and under worked for ten and twelve and even fourteen hours a day, or longer at rush seasons. "The employers," Florence Kelley observed, "are ashamed of hiring children and cannot bring themselves to report the full number."

It has been mentioned that under the sweatshop system no attempt was made to guard against the spread of disease by germs carried away on finished garments. A case of smallpox had developed among the foreign colony at the World's Fair. It had not been reported, with the result that the disease was spreading and threatening the whole city. Its ravages would obviously be worst among the poor people in the huddled tenements, in the sweatshops. No effort had been made at quarantine, only a sign on a door or window told of smallpox within. Garments were passing through the working places with smallpox next door, in the rooms above and below, even in the tenement where the work was actually going on. Worse, garments were going out to the general trade with no warning of what they carried.

Florence Kelley and her workers set themselves to find where these contaminated objects were and stop their circulation. She knew herself of one coat in a certain workplace where smallpox was immediately present. She went to find it and discovered that it was gone. Relentlessly, she pursued it and finally caught up with it several tenement houses away, where it was seized and destroyed. There had been one case of smallpox in the house where it was originally deposited; now there were four.

By her energy and her authority Miss Kelley managed to get the proper regulations revived and enforced, and hundreds of dollars' worth of garments were seized and destroyed. But smallpox was not the only disease that was being spread by the sweatshops. There were also typhoid and tuberculosis. And so many children worked in the shops that the germs of measles, scarlet fever, whooping cough and other ailments were everywhere threatening those more fortunate youngsters who were to wear the garments in far different surroundings.

One might think that Hull House would have become a

dismal place with all these reports being brought in daily, accounts of the horrors and abuses in the sweatshops which were everywhere. This was far from the case. Those who were closest to Jane Addams, the brilliant group that was gathering about her, saw only challenge and no discouragement in all that was going on. Julia Lathrop and Florence Kelley were remarkable talkers. Julia with her nimble wit, Florence with her truculent arguments, Jane with her steady good sense, Mary Rozet Smith her quiet wisdom — over and over again they reviewed the situation before them, summed up the conditions of which they alone were so fully aware. Something must be done.

To press for public recognition of and a general sentiment against these flaming abuses was now, they decided, far from enough. Even pressure by trade unions, with recourse to the devastating weapon of strikes, could not hope to bring permanent reform. The only real remedy must come from the law, a law that could and would be enforced, that would banish, by higher authority, these flourishing conditions of social injustice.

To achieve such a law would be a very difficult task. Child labor was in great demand. Children's quickness to learn, their nimble fingers, and their rapidity of action were all of definite value. But to work young children to such an extent that they lost their health and strength before they were really grown, to keep them out of school before they got even the rudiments of learning, would in the end result in the raising up of a whole generation of illiterates, who would never be able to rise above a certain level of efficiency. They would be a drag on society for all their lives. Not only in decency and fairness, but in common sense such an end should not be risked in modern civilized society. Jane knew that other people besides the Hull House group must also feel this, for there are many decent people in the world. They must be found, organized and marshaled for a struggle.

Jane and her associates, clubwomen and patrons of Hull House, went forth to speak everywhere in the challenging campaign for fair labor practice. It was for all workers, especially children. The women speakers were able, and their cause convincing, which was suddenly proved with startling plainness.

A masculine friend of Jane's and of Hull House asked her one day to lunch at the Union League Club to meet two gentlemen who wished to discuss with her what they referred to as the sweatshop bill. They proved to be representatives of an informal association of manufacturers, a body not very numerous but of undoubted power. Conversation, after due openings were got through, was brought round to the subject in question and Jane was told baldly that if the residents of Hull House would give up this nonsense about sweatshops of which these women knew nothing, certain businessmen were prepared to put at their disposal a gift of fifty thousand dollars, to be completed in two years, which would, as they suggested, "make Hull House the largest institution on the West Side."

Jane was about to answer in a white heat of refusal when a thought pushed itself into her mind. What was it that a Chicago newspaper editor had said of her father after he died? It was that John Addams was the one man of whom it could be said that he had never even been offered a bribe because of his known integrity.

"What had befallen the daughter of such a man," she reflected, "that such a thing should happen to her?" She pulled herself together and answered humbly but with full firmness. The acceptance of such an offer, she declared, would be impossible. Hull House had no ambition to be the largest institution on the West Side, but, on the contrary, would rather be reduced to ruin than to prosper by such means. "That much heroics," she tells us, "youth did permit itself." The friend who had been the intermediary here interrupted the difficult conversation and the ill-advised luncheon came to an end.

Jane could indulge herself with the thought that her situation was most unlike that of her father. Here was an instance of huge moneyed interests being involved in a time and at a place in which corruption flourished completely unchecked, and when honor in business matters was at so low a premium that none of the gentlemen present thought of the proposed transaction as anything irregular.

There was daily discussion at Hull House about what the proposed legislation should cover. The immediate needs were positive and endless. There should be relief of women workers from night employment by which, on account of the unavoidable daytime duties of most women, they were apt to be completely exhausted. There should be insurance against the sudden laying off of employees when business slackened, as it did sometimes by seasons, sometimes by unpredictable changes in the condition of the market. Had not the Hard Times, now passing away, given a sharp lesson in that possibility? Was that lesson to be so soon forgotten? There should be other labor insurance also to provide help in time of sickness or in case of accidents, to guarantee security in old age. One question crowded upon another, but if a proper law were to be formulated, it would not be wise to ask for too much. To achieve the first real regulation must be the main purpose. The law must be simple and not too difficult to enforce.

It was clear enough to Jane that her former popularity in Chicago had by now diminished to almost nothing. George Pullman, once her good friend, had turned upon her completely on account of her stand at the time of the strike. Other men in his position did the same thing; her defense of the trade unions made her seem not only mistaken but dangerous. The newspapers were heavily against her; they were calling her a "radical." None of this deterred her.

The fact had to be faced that there would be fierce, even merciless opposition to the new legislation which Hull House was preparing to support. The presence of children in industry was a thing too highly profitable to be given up without a struggle. There were some who said that whole industries would collapse if children could not be employed. Hull House had an answer to that. "Would you save a man's wages by overworking a child?" To many heads of businesses it was unthinkable that money must be paid out to make better working conditions so that young people just coming to maturity would not be choked by bad air, or their backs permanently bent from working over clumsy, heavy, and dangerous machines. Reason and justice and human mercy were all on the side of those who were working for a factory law, but well-entrenched power was established on the other side.

The women of Hull House and their broad circle of friends planned, consulted, and sought legal advice. Jane was a shrewd campaigner. A delegation would go to Springfield to lay their plan before the governor, but it must not be made up of representatives of Hull House alone. The trade unions must have their part also; from them Jane expected firm support. And the richer and more influential women, those members of clubs who had taken up this cause of a better labor law — they also must help present the plan.

Slowly the wording of the law took shape. Lawyers, professors at the University of Chicago, other wise friends, contributed their advice. The time came to carry it to the capital and ask for help from Governor Altgeld. The small and oddly assorted party set out with high hope.

IX

John Altgeld and the Work
and Factory Law of 1893

The capital city of Springfield, seeming so small and remote from roaring Chicago, was full of reminders of Abraham Lincoln, and of Jane's father, who had so admired
him. She had tried to carry over that same sense of admiration and understanding to her boys at Hull House. In every
way that she and Mary Rozet Smith could devise, the
members of the Hero Club had been made familiar with
that Illinois hero who came from the common people and
had them always in his heart. There was much to fill Jane's
mind as the little delegation waited to be shown into the
presence of the governor.

Political corruption in the Republican party in Chicago
had become so brazen that when the campaign for governor
came up in 1892 the Democrats, long out of office, managed to elect a candidate of their own. He was John Peter
Altgeld, born in Germany and brought to this country
when he was still a baby. He proved himself the able and
fearless man for whom the voters had hoped, although his

administration was a greatly troubled one, burdened at the beginning by the Hard Times. As newly elected governor, Altgeld had ridden in the same carriage with President Cleveland at the opening of the World's Fair on May 1, 1893. They treated each other with cool politeness, for even then there was no love lost between them, in spite of their being fellow Democrats. That was before the blazing quarrel which arose when Cleveland insisted, against Altgeld's objections, on bringing in federal troops at the time of the Pullman strikes.

John Altgeld listened with earnest attention as the little company that stood before his desk set forth their views and explained what they hoped their law would do. Briefly they outlined its terms to the new governor:

No child under fourteen years of age was to be employed in any manufacturing establishment, factory, or workshop within the state. The employer must keep a record of all children, their ages, addresses and abilities; this record to be open to inspectors, like Florence Kelley and Julia Lathrop, at all times.

Children, along with affidavits from their parents as to their ages, must also present a statement of their own that they had attended school up to the age of fourteen and could read and write in English.

No woman was to be required to work more than eight hours a day, or more than six days a week. In other words, if she was a sweatshop worker, she was not to undertake a double amount of finishing and take it home on Saturday to complete on Sunday.

The terms of the law do not seem very drastic now, but for the time they were staggering. The demand for an eight-hour day was raised again when everyone had insisted that

the Haymarket riot had killed it. The age limit of fourteen
years for children had been vaguely defined earlier; here was
stern notice that it would now be enforced. Children who
did not seem physically equal to the work they were doing,
even if they were of the proper age, must be examined by a
doctor if the inspector said so, and get a certificate stating
that they were in proper health.

Florence Kelley's first inspections had been so thorough
and her reports forwarded to the legislature had been so
convincing that a commission was appointed to examine
the real condition of Chicago workers. The commission
came in a body to dine at Hull House and heard still more
of how bad things were. They went away convinced. Hope
rode very high on Halstead Street.

The bill came up in the legislature in May of 1893, was
discussed, argued, wrangled over. Hull House waited
breathlessly. At last the joyful news arrived from Springfield that it had passed. There had been plenty of opposition to it; pressure had been brought to bear on the
governor, but he had refused to be moved. His influence
was potent and had saved the bill. He signed it into law on
June 17, 1893, a date momentous indeed for the Hull
House community. Nine days later there was to come a
date even more momentous but of that they were still
happily unconscious.

It seemed at first that a great permanent victory had
been won. Governor Altgeld immediately appointed Florence Kelley chief inspector for the Factory Law to see to its
enforcement. Mrs. Kelley was made for just such an office.
The situation cried for a person like her. She was empowered to bring charges against anyone found violating
the new regulations; here was a battlefield worthy of her

steel. Various employers had decided not to be disturbed by the new law. They thought they could evade it easily enough, for laws in Illinois and particularly in Chicago were, if unpopular, for the most part unenforced. They did not know Florence Kelley!

She excelled in plain speaking. She tackled Marshall Field about his employing young boys to run errands back and forth in the giant store. Why were they not in school? She descended into foul cellars or climbed to rickety attics to observe the conditions in the sweatshops being operated there. She was deaf to the pleas of parents who were bound that their children of ten and eleven should go to work to help support them, pehaps to keep a worthless father in drink. She and her assistants seemed to be everywhere; certainly they saw everything. Governor Altgeld had good reason to be satisfied with his appointment when he observed what was going on in relation to the new law. But he could not spare the time for constant observation.

A great outcry had arisen among those who had supported Altgeld's election. The moneyed men of Chicago, having grown tired of being fleeced in every contract and franchise by the petty politicians of the city and state government, had come forward to stand for cleaner politics. But they had not bargained on this move to regulate and to restrict child labor, which threatened to cut down their profits. It was not for this that they had put John Altgeld into office! The lesser politicians were already furious with him for having begun at once to clean up the graft, the plundering of the city moneys, the police protection of gambling houses. Altgeld's name was becoming unpopular on all sides. Now, with his stand to improve the condition of the workers, there was criticism of him everywhere as of Jane Addams. Worse was to come.

The affair of the Haymarket Riot seven years before had cut so deep into Chicago's memory that there was no forgetting it. The members of the Amnesty Association were still bringing to each succeeding governor their plea for clemency, though only three of the condemned men were now left alive in prison. Usually the arguments for reversing the sentences had been on the basis of mercy alone. But Governor Altgeld was a lawyer — he had been a judge of the Illinois Superior Court — and he approached the matter from a different point of view. When appealed to, he agreed to go over the records of the trial held before Judge Gary and see if the verdict should be reconsidered.

Altgeld had brought himself up from the position of a poor immigrant boy. He had studied law and had risen to be a very successful jurist and politician. Possibly his ambitions might have led him to hope for even higher honors than governor of Illinois — a place in the Senate, perhaps, or in the United States Supreme Court. He told a friend that it would be political suicide for him to pardon these men, but if he were convinced from the records that they were innocent, nothing could hold him back.

He went over every word of the trial records, noting where the presiding judge had flouted all order of law and procedure, had treated the men as condemned already, how fully he had connived in a packed jury. He investigated the conduct of the police during the labor disputes which led up to the Haymarket Riot. Then he declared his final opinion that the bomb had been thrown in secret individual revenge by someone who had been undeservedly clubbed and beaten by the police. On June 26, 1893 he pardoned all three and ended his public declaration with an excoriating attack on Judge Gary.

The resulting clamor of abuse which arose about him went up to the very clouds. The familiar cry of anarchist was raised; he was denounced as a public menace. It was quite obvious that he had committed political suicide. Through it all Jane Addams was his firm supporter and friend. She regretted his scathing denunciation of Judge Gary but did not claim that it was unfounded.

From the beginning of his administration Altgeld maintained that relief of the poor should be the responsibility of the government. Under him much had been done for social betterment which his enemies set themselves busily to undo. He had lived in Joliet, the site of the great state penitentiary. There he had studied prison methods and published a small book, *Our Penal Machinery and Its Victims*. Among other things, he pointed out what desperate harm is done to young delinquents by imprisoning them, even for twenty-four hours, with hardened criminals.

After his first term he ran for governor once more but there was no hope of his being elected. He was never returned to any elective office. His business affairs, which once seemed to prosper, came to ruin. Jealousy and hatred were poured out upon him for the rest of his life by those who had sought to use him for their own ends and had failed. But Jane Addams always stood by him. Not for nothing had she learned from her father to be true to her own integrity.

That integrity was being put under heavy pressure at this time, even from those closest about her. She had reason to recall the days when Miss Sill was determined that she should be a missionary and she, determined to be true to herself, had resisted. She was being urged now to become a declared socialist; there were at hand many headlong young thinkers who insisted that this was the answer to all the existing vexed questions.

Florence Kelley was an ardent socialist, although she had been expelled from the party. Ellen Gates Starr, founder of Hull House with Jane, was one. Julia Lathrop had leaned toward socialism once but had turned away from it. A number of those taking part in Hull House affairs, especially in the Working People's Social Science Club, insisted that Jane should embrace socialism. Some even insisted that, with her liberal views, she actually was a socialist already.

Socialism was very much in the air then among the trade unions and among the young instructors at the new University of Chicago. But Jane thought of Miss Sill and held her ground. It was true that many of the old and traditional views were cracking and showing their inadequacy in a new age, but solid good sense kept her within the bounds of her own considered reasons. Florence Kelley was an indefatigable arguer, but she did not prevail. It is to be said for Mrs. Kelley that divergence of view from her colleagues made no difference to her nor had any influence on her loyalty and affection.

It can well be imagined what rejoicing there was at Hull House when the Work and Factory Bill of 1893 was passed. Many plans were laid to make the most of it, and for further legislation which this first factory law did not cover. The Eight Hours Club was formed for women workers who read all the literature on the subject and helped seek the public support necessary to make the law effective.

The campaign in support of the Factory Law had cul-minated during the very difficult year of 1893 when em-ployment fell to such a low level and with the laboring population in such distress. Strikes were many and violent. Employers were also anguished concerning the unpredict-able nature of the market, and thus were all the more on edge when they saw what they thought were completely un-informed women meddling in vitally important affairs. Their own policy was basically shortsighted, thoroughly against any change. Someone pointed out the possible ad-vantage to the garment trade if power sewing machines could be introduced and work done at a central factory. The answer was, "We have found it cheaper to use sweaters and foot-powered machines." It was expensive cheapness but they were not able to see so far.

These men, masters of manufacturing and trading estab-lishments, did not in truth represent the whole employer class of Chicago. They had no very large body of associates, but they were well organized and firmly set in their tradi-tions. They paid the highest taxes, and through the weight of their advertising, they had the ear of the press and could exert great strength in opposition to any move toward control of working conditions. Many sober and solid for-tunes were being made in Chicago by decent and sensible men, but a good many even of these were singularly blind to what was going on around them. They were also rather irresponsibly prone to listen to and repeat those frequently aired remarks about Jane Addams being a "dangerous radical."

The spirit of vilification is apt to be contagious and denunciation of her and the ways of Hull House was growing ever wider. It is to be remembered that her real

friends stood steadily by her and a great many others reserved judgment for the time at least. Nevertheless, as
weeks passed, as difficult times and strikes continued, she
was well aware that her standing in the public eye was
falling lower and lower. Yet her purposes did not change.

One of Jane's most effective helpers came to join forces
with Hull House during the battle to enforce the Work
and Factory Law. Louise DeKoven Bowen, Mrs. Joseph
Bowen, said she had grown up with Chicago and was
neither blinded by its glittering prosperity nor frustrated by
the appalling problems which industrial poverty presented.
She early showed ability in women's club affairs, and had
become prominent in the various women's organizations of
which Chicago society was full.

She greatly admired Jane Addams and came to Hull
House to discover how she could be of service. She could
see at once how much the Hull House Women's Club
meant to its members, yet how inexperienced they were in
managing their affairs and their meetings. They were completely inexpert in parliamentary order, finding it difficult
to complete their main business on account of getting
involved in smaller issues along the way. Mrs. Bowen asked
Jane to put her name up for membership at one of the next
meetings, feeling sure that when she was enrolled she could
help them greatly. There was nothing in the least officious
about this suggestion; she was honestly aware that they
needed help, and she was just as honestly certain that she
could give it.

When the day for election of new members came,
Louise Bowen was at Hull House in good time so that she
could take her place at once. An hour passed, and the
painful fact developed that she had not been elected! The

women may have been afraid of her, since she came from a world so different from theirs — may have felt themselves awkward and inadequate in the face of her greater social ease and sophisticated presence.

She did not for a moment resent this unexpected failure of her plans, but understood completely how the women felt, and set herself to put the situation right. She knew how to make people feel at ease, how to win confidence, how to show vital interest in their lives, how to meet them halfway when they timidly responded to overtures of friendship. In no time at all, in spite of her wealth, in spite of her confident efficiency, the women all came to appreciate her, then to be devoted to her. She and they had one basic thing in common. They loved Jane Addams and would do anything for her. Louise Bowen became president of the Women's Club and held that office for seventeen years. The incident confirmed again Jane Addams's belief that you "had to know people before you could help them." Louise Bowen had successfully crossed the bridge between two ways of life which George Pullman had been unable to pass.

Mrs. Bowen did not join the residents on Halstead Street, having her own busy life to live in her own place in Chicago. But she became an energetic and moving force in all Hull House affairs. As treasurer of the board of trustees she brought her able financial sense to the intricacies of the Hull House budget and the task of supporting all its greatly needed and rapidly multiplying activities.

Florence Kelley's work continued with unsparing vigor. She was empowered as part of her office to bring legal charges wherever she found gross infractions. When she took one of her complaints to the young district attorney, he said in surprise, "You don't expect me to take such a case do you?" To which she responded that she emphatically did. He declared that his office was so busy he could not reach the matter in question for at least two years. She left him in disgust, went straight to the offices of Northwestern University's Law School and enrolled for night study. Henceforth she would take care of the ins and outs of legal matters herself. She completed her course and was admitted to the bar, but never practiced. She had only meant to arm herself for further battle.

One curious regulation came to light during this period of drastic examination of industrial conditions. The law, it seemed, permitted that a child well under fourteen years of age could get authority to work if he was the sole support of a dependent parent. An affidavit had to be offered that the situation was genuine. It could be signed by the parents or by the child himself and could easily be fraudulent. Picture a child of eleven, twelve, or thirteen years of age working for the living of himself and a helpless father or mother. What would be the level of subsistence of that unfortunate family?

There was anxious indignation and questioning over the existence of such a regulation until Mrs. Bowen, with her firm good sense, suggested that there should be investigation of just how many cases existed at the moment. The answer, after careful searching, proved to be that there were no more than ten or twelve. For these working children Louise Bowen raised among her friends scholarships of sufficient amount so that the children could have the support of the income and still go to school. Hopefully they and the dependent parents lived better by this means than by the children's own efforts.

Louise Bowen and her husband Joseph Bowen were

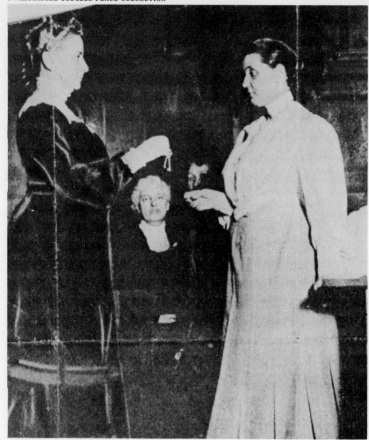

Louise Bowen presenting an anniversary gift to Jane Addams

untiringly generous to Hull House, knowing to the full its
needs. Following the gift by Mary Rozet Smith of a building for the children, Mrs. Bowen gave one for the women's
clubs, with a large floor space for general meetings. Her
husband added to this a building for the boys' clubs, with a
gymnasium and workshops for metalwork and carpentry.
On the day it was due to be opened, Mr. Bowen was sweep-

[140]

ing the walk in front of the door and Jane was giving a last polish to the stairs when the boys came trooping in.

The period of Florence Kelley's investigations was to end abruptly. But before it was over she had weighed all the elements that went into the existence of sweatshops and studied them with penetrating insight. She concluded that there was no real remedy for the evils these shops engendered except to bring the whole system to an end. She enumerated the number of sweatshops, thousands of them, in operation in Chicago alone, and reported that they were constantly failing and going out of business, then coming into being again at another address or under another name. It was manifestly impossible ever to give them full and honest inspection. They must go!

The Work and Factory Law came into being in June 1893. It passed out of existence somewhat more than a year later, in March 1895. With the hostility to it in high places it was bound to be tested by law sooner or later. An employer named Ritchie was charged with working a woman for more than eight hours in a single day and was fined five dollars. The amount was insignificant but the purpose was large. He appealed the case to the Supreme Court of Illinois and the judgment was reversed, the law was pronounced unconstitutional. The court declared that it "was unable to find any reasonable connection between the limitation of hours and the public welfare." The Factory Law, the court finally pronounced, "denied women their fundamental and inalienable rights of freedom of contract," and the law's brief term came to an end. There were stout hearts at Hull House, but the blow was a very heavy one.

When John Altgeld went out of office, his successor

removed Florence Kelley and her twelve assistants from their work of inspection. But the efforts of Mrs. Kelley and those of her helpers had been so thorough, and her vigorous publicity regarding working conditions had been so effective that she had good right to say, "At least, the sweat-shops are never going to be the same again."

One of the residents at Hull House evolved a saying: "Sometimes there is nothing to do but to keep on keeping on." That was what Hull House would now proceed to do.

X

Especially for Children

It is not to be imagined that Jane Addams and her associates spent any time in lamentation over the annihilation of their Work and Factory Law by the Illinois Supreme Court. Theirs was a gay and gallant company. They were all buoyant of spirit and sure that the future held challenge and no threat of final failure. Jane, Florence Kelley, Julia Lathrop and Ellen Starr were all within a year or two of the same age. Mary Rozet Smith was much younger, Mrs. Bowen somewhat older. They had plenty of time and opportunity before them and six years of Hull House success to reassure them. It was difficult even to keep up with the work there, which seemed to grow of itself. There was a music school now, and an art school, as well as all the rapidly multiplying classes and clubs.

When she left Rockford, Ellen Gates Starr began a quiet and conventional life much like that which she had lived in a small midwestern town, but in these new surroundings she suddenly blossomed out into a different person. She became a declared socialist. She picketed on strike lines, she marched in processions, she spoke on street corners. Her activity in support of women's unions was untiring nor was she afraid of disapproving policemen.

Yet Ellen Starr never lost sight of the original and basic interest in her life. It was to pursue beauty, to teach others to see it, most especially to add some measure of it to the drab and ugly households that crowded so close around Hull House. She had conducted classes in art appreciation at the fashionable North Side School for Girls, where she had been a teacher before she joined Jane at Hull House. It was due to her that the first additional building, added to Hull House in 1891 was the Butler Picture Gallery.

Edward Butler was a director of the Chicago Art Institute and a well-established merchant. He believed in pictures and beauty as Ellen Starr did. The two architect brothers Pond and Pond were enlisted. They began a course of construction, as one building after another was added, that made a most fortunate whole and in time covered the entire block, built around a court in the middle like Toynbee Hall. Miss Culver, the former owner, became so impressed with what Hull House was accomplishing that she gave the whole parcel of land upon which it stood to the enterprise in "perpetual lease."

The Butler Gallery had a reading room on the first floor and an exhibition hall boldly designed with modern lighting and arrangement. Above was a studio where art classes were held. The immigrant neighbors made immediate and enthusiastic use of the gift. They knew about picture galleries; in the crowded European cities from which they had come, pictures were among the few things that poor people could afford to enjoy.

No attempt was made to gather and own a collection of

art treasures. Loan exhibitions were held; volunteers came to teach the classes in drawing, painting and sculpture. Promising young artists were discovered among the candidates that came flocking to the doors. Many times tragedy was enacted when an especially gifted young person was compelled by family needs to give up all hope of an artistic career at the age of sixteen and enter the four walls of a place of work which would be his prison for the rest of his life. But at least he would have Hull House to come to still. Outside Hull House, Ellen Starr interested herself in loan exhibits for the public schools and initiated the Public School Art Society.

Late in the autumn that followed the termination of the Factory Law, a real shadow fell upon Hull House. Jane Addams was severely, even desperately ill. Although her letters or reminiscences do not speak of ill health, she was actually a frail person, with a number of serious illnesses and a series of operations from which she rose indomitably to go to work again. This time she came nearer to death than in any sickness before, for she had contracted typhoid fever. She always maintained that she had got the germ somewhere else and that nothing concerning Hull House was to blame.

When she finally began to recover, her doctor said that a long vacation away from Hull House and its cares was imperatively necessary. It was decided that she and Mary Rozet Smith would go abroad for several months in a leisurely journey about Europe. Because of her Russian neighbors and their complex problems, Jane was most anxious to see what she could of their country and their way of life. Her most important goal was Yasnaya Polyana, the home and estate of Count Leo Tolstoy. He was at that time probably the most famous novelist in the world, but more important to Jane were his views on social matters and on democracy, on the contribution of humble people to the scheme of things, and the need for other people to share it.

At his country place Tolstoy lived and dressed and worked like a peasant. He received many visitors there whom the Countess Tolstoy entertained with the ordinary comforts of life, but he and his daughter worked daily in the fields and ate nothing but the coarsest peasant fare. In his *Anna Karenina* there is an unforgettable scene where the hero, Levin, works all day reaping in the fields with his serfs, and feels his cares and problems fall away as he does so. What attracted Jane to Tolstoy, after she had read all of his work that was within her reach, was his belief in "getting off the backs of the poor." He protested against the czarist system of society of that day, in which the privileged class drew abundant wealth from the labors of the huge, toiling, underprivileged poor.

The itinerary of the two travelers took them first to London, where Jane made at once for Toynbee Hall and her friends Canon and Mrs. Barnett and their companions, who had taught her so much when she was first planning the venture of Hull House. In Moscow, where they went next, they met Aylmer Maude, the translator of Tolstoy's novels. It was he who escorted them to Yasnaya Polyana.

The visit to the great man was a trifle disappointing, for he did not seem to warm to Jane Addams and the work she was doing as did almost everyone else who knew her. It was the fashion of the moment for women's dresses to have sleeves that were not only large but enormous. At their first interview Tolstoy pulled out the stuff of one of hers to its full extent and commented that there was enough material on one arm to make a child a dress. He asked why she did not dress like the people she was aiming to help, and she replied, unquenched, that the working girls she knew had even bigger sleeves, and they would think there was something queer about her if she did not dress like other people. He bluntly asked her what was the source of her income, her "food and shelter." It happened that the largest investment of property that her father had bequeathed to her was an extensive and now rented farm in Wisconsin, left to her and her sisters.

When she explained this to him he replied, "So you are an absentee landlord! Do you think you will help the people more by adding to the crowded city than you would by tilling your own soil?"

This was scarcely a reasonable suggestion. Jane very sensibly said of him afterward that "he was more logical than life warrants," nor did she try now to explain to him how unlike their positions were and how essentially different their tasks in life. He made great emphasis in all his teaching upon the idea that "bread labor," the kind of toil that produces the basic necessities of life, was more important than anything else. This she did accept in good faith and made up her mind that when she got back to Chicago she would conscientiously give two hours a day to "bread labor" in the bakery of the Hull House Coffee Shop.

She wondered a little, being an American housewife, how the trade union of her German baker was going to take this, but she kept the resolution in her mind all through the rest of her travels. She would be able to carry it out very literally, for her father, being a miller, had always insisted that when each of his daughters was twelve years old she must be able to produce a perfect loaf. She arrived back in

Chicago in due time, still determined to carry out the impulse to do good works directly in the form of the simplest of good deeds.

When she saw on the first day how much was waiting for her, the letters to be answered, the problems to meet, the people who had been hopefully looking to her for comfort and advice, she realized in an instant how impractical was the idea of letting everything else go while "I saved my soul by two hours' work at baking bread." The whole plan, she concluded, was a preposterous one, just as long ago she had known how preposterous it was for her to believe that her father was ashamed of her. She was too humble-minded to think that she knew more of certain subjects than the great Count Leo Tolstoy. At least they were both pursuing the same ends, that of understanding poverty and in good time doing away with it.

It was a shock to see that industry, after the reversal of the Factory Law, had gone back to its old practices. But with renewed energy and courage after her long holiday, she set herself to the task of seeing what could be done. It was plain that in the interval of more than a year while the Factory Law was in operation some lasting change for the better had been brought about. Florence Kelley was still certain that the sweatshops would never be quite the same again, although this fell far short of her dictum that for any real solution of the problem, they must be done away with entirely. The enforcement of what regulations still existed concerning child labor now demanded so much paperwork that some employers did not care to get involved in it and ceased to hire children. There must be more accumulation of the facts about overworked women and the employment of young children, Jane Addams decided. Because of her careful study and her revelation of various practices of which an unheeding public had never heard, she was beginning to be referred to as one of the highest authorities on child labor.

Florence Kelley, discharged after Altgeld went out of office, had been succeeded by a man who had worked twenty-five years in the glass factories at Alton, the place where the conditions of child labor were the most outrageous of any that had been brought to light. The boys' work in a typical glass establishment was in shifts from 2:30 A.M. to 2:30 P.M., half night and half day, or with alternating night and day work. When an inspector remonstrated against such a schedule as totally unfit for growing boys, the answer was, "Well, what are we going to do about it? We can't waste the glass!" The boys were taken as early as the age of ten.

Mrs. Kelley was about to leave Hull House, having been drafted by special messenger to come to New York and act as executive secretary for the newly formed Consumers' League. The Chicago system was not to look upon her like again. She had, therefore, no direct part in the next movement with which Hull House was to be concerned, the creation of the Juvenile Court.

The temptations which lay all about the very young in this time and place, the opportunities for juvenile crime, were never-ending. Along the edges of the railroad yards bits of coal often lay scattered by accident from the switching coal cars. Children would be sent out with bags to pick it up and carry it home where it was a greatly needed source of fuel. This was legal enough, but it was only one small step to obtaining it more easily from the coal piles dumped outside stores by delivery trucks.

It was equally easy to purloin fruit and vegetables from outdoor racks or pushcarts. When one is cold and hungry, with half-frozen, mittenless hands, neither of these acts seems very blameworthy in itself. But such thievery can amount to serious losses for small businesses hard-driven by competition, and can also lead to greater thefts. Picking pockets has to be an acquired accomplishment, but it is not difficult to learn if there is a good teacher at hand. Flipping streetcars is against the law, but a challenging pastime. Empty buildings invite smashed windows and breaking and entering. There are innumerable ways for the young to get themselves into trouble with the law.

The plays in the local theaters were just as sensational and suggestive of crime and violence as many of the movies are today. If the police arrested a child or an adolescent, there was nothing to do with him but to put him into the city jail where he shared quarters with professional criminals. He was tried in the police courts and if committed to prison was at once in daily company that was even worse than in the jail.

Sometimes his parents were fined, or if they could not pay, the young delinquent must work it out in prison at fifty cents a day. Many judges simply let the accused child go, feeling that prison would be the ruin of him and that it was too cruel to lay fines on hard-working parents who could not possibly meet them. The convicted child usually came out of prison at the end of his sentence more hardened and more inclined to lawbreaking than when he went in, for he was at the formative age when a boy or girl learns easily and is very apt at imitation.

There was a great demand in the factories for young boys in their teens, for they were valuable on assembly lines and in tending machines. When they poured out of the factory doors at the end of long monotonous hours of doing the same trivial thing over and over again, they were ready to embrace any chance at diversion and brief pleasure. There were plenty of experienced tempters close at hand, ready to exploit this need for the sake of unlawful gain, which often ended in the boy's arrest and accusation of disorderly behavior because an outraged policeman did not know what else to do.

Even before Hull House was founded, the Chicago Women's Clubs had begun to make some slow progress toward improvements in the jail system. They had got the filthy living conditions remedied to a certain but not very large degree, they had introduced women matrons and had organized a school for children arrested for truancy and for boys awaiting trial or serving short sentences in jail. But that had not been enough. The dreadful adult company to which both boys and girls were exposed remained the same.

There was also the problem of dependent children whose parents were dead or had deserted them, or more simply were unable to support them. Where were they to go? Not to the poorhouses among the senile and the imbecile; that at least had been made plain by such investigators as Julia Lathrop. The county maintained certain industrial schools, but judges hesitated to send children there since the county was often unwilling to carry even that small cost of supporting them. Public opinion began to be organized for a court that could deal with children's problems separately and specifically.

Jane Addams said in regard to her young neighbors who fell into trouble with the law, "Our problems are not to be worked out in the school but in the streets." It was plain

to those at Hull House and to various members of the
Chicago Women's Club, under the leadership of Mrs.
Bowen and a Mrs. Lucy Flower, that some better plan for
delinquent young people must be discovered. Lawyers interested in the proper administration of justice were concerned with the same thing. It was Judge Harvey B. Hurd
who succeeded in drafting a measure which could and did
successfully survive the test as to whether or not it was
constitutional, and passed into law. Its title was "An Act to
Regulate the Treatment and Control of Dependent, Neglected and Delinquent Children."

Mrs. Lucy Flower was one of the earnest backers of the
bill. It was she who formed the Juvenile Court Committee
of which Julia Lathrop was the first president, and Mrs.
Joseph Bowen a powerful member. After the state legislature had passed the measure in 1899, they set themselves to
see that it was carried out.

Proceedings were now to be entirely different. Where
there had been a crowded courtroom with idle spectators
wandering in and out, arguing lawyers and a judge aloof
from the bewildered and incoherent young offender in the
prisoner's dock, now there would be a quiet room with no
one present except those directly concerned. The judge, a
kindly understanding man, would be on one side of a table,
the young offender on the other with his parents and two
members of the Juvenile Court Committee.

There would be interested questions and warm encour-
agement to give full and clear answers. Results achieved
could be quite different, too. This was an examination, not
a trial. If the questioning revealed that the offender must
be kept under surveillance for a time, there was to be a
detention home for him — clean, quiet, with decent food

and without the aspects of a prison. On one occasion a group of boys had been arrested because they had been digging a cave under a busy thoroughfare, which they persisted in enlarging, with great danger of collapse of the roadway. As they were taken away to the place of detention they asked wistfully if there were not someplace round about where they could safely dig themselves another underground domicile. Boys under arrest remained boys still.

The real heart of the plan for the Juvenile Court was the probation system, whereby each offender, after being questioned, studied, and held if necessary for further observation, was finally released in the charge of a probation officer who would thenceforward be responsible for him or her. But in the interest of getting it passed, the original draft of the law had provided no funds for salaries of probation officers. These were necessary, since few people could afford to give sufficient time and attention to such a task without some return. Furthermore, while it was decreed that no children should again be committed to a county jail or a state prison, no building was set aside to be used for a detention home. It was necessary to pass a second bill through the legislature to fill these needs.

The vote for this second bill, in contrast to others like the Work and Factory Law which had been so long delayed, was accomplished with breathtaking speed. Mrs. Bowen had a friend who sat in the state legislature. She asked him to dinner one night and put the draft of the subsidiary bill before him. He at once, in her presence, called up the House of Representatives at Springfield and asked to speak to a man who was acknowledged to be the "boss" of that body. On being told of the bill this man evidently asked at the other end of the telephone line "What's in it?" The reply was, "There's nothing in it, but a woman I know wants it passed." It was duly passed. Illinois politics could occasionally be as simple as that.

Among the able and understanding judges who saw the Juvenile Court through its beginnings was Judge Julian Mack, a jurist distinguished in many branches of legal achievement. It was he who explained the real essence of the change which the court had brought about: "It was the conception that a child that broke the law was to be dealt with by the state as a wise parent would deal with a wayward child." There was no idea of punishment or of frightening the offender to prevent his doing the same again. It was a matter of understanding him and what had got him into trouble, of accomplishing a cure, not of inflicting a penalty. The Juvenile Court in Chicago came into being in 1899, almost simultaneously with the one founded in Denver, Colorado, by Judge Ben Lindsay.

A number of probation officers were among the residents of Hull House, where they could and did talk over all the possibilities and problems of the new system of probation. There they had access to Mary Smith's careful wisdom, which everyone partook of and deeply respected. She was devoted to children and knew how to understand them as few others did. Julia Lathrop's keen knowledge of human nature, sharpened by her experience in investigating all the state charity institutions of Illinois, threw light on much that would otherwise have been bewildering in the situations which had to be met. Most potent of all was Jane Addams's deep conviction of the importance of youth, of its right to free development and its cravings and its needs.

Much came out of those discussions which would be of value in all future activities of the court.

For reasons that it is difficult to divine, the idea of the Juvenile Court, so easily accepted by the state legislature, met with mean, stubborn hostility from Chicago's county and city governments, from the aldermen, the police organization, the departments of construction and repair, even from the mayor. It was here that Mrs. Bowen and Julia Lathrop showed their mettle and their valiant determination not to accept defeat.

The county government at first made no effort to set aside a building as a place of detention, as they were supposed to do. So the committee had to find one. The city government allowed its management eleven cents a day for food for each child, and undertook to provide transportation to and from the court building where the children had to go for examination. The transportation consisted of a rickety old omnibus, drawn by a small and ancient horse which was plainly quite unequal to any such task.

The committee asked for another steed and were finally granted an ancient firehorse which had been retired. He pulled so hard when harnessed with the small one that he pulled the poor little creature off its legs and almost strangled it. The committee finally raised the money to buy a pair of horses. When they asked for a stable they were offered one four miles away and were obliged to rent one close by. It was supposed that the city or county would pay for the horses' feed but there was not even eleven cents a day for that and the committee shouldered this expense also.

The matter of the omnibus was something else again. It

was in such bad repair that the driver came in one day to report some of the boards had fallen out of the bottom and he had almost lost the children out of it. Mrs. Bowen went to the county office to ask for repairs but was told that this was a city responsibility and that she would have to see the chief of police. She went to his office, where she waited, standing, in a room so crowded with men that there was no seat for her. All of them seemed amused at the sight of a woman, a lady in fact, waiting to see the chief of police. She waited all day. At dark it was found that he had slipped out by a side door and gone home.

Undefeated, Mrs. Bowen and Julia Lathrop returned the next day. He did see them then and told them that the omnibus was not his affair; they must see the repair department. There the omnibus was declared too far gone to be used again, and they were told to apply to the construction department. From there they were sent to the mayor, who sent them to the county commissioners who sent them to . . . This is called in political circles "being given the runaround," a known effective treatment for the most persistent applications. The committee finally bought their own omnibus and horses, rented their own stables and provided their own horse feed.

They had good luck, however, in finding the perfect superintendent for their Detention Home. She was a little old lady of over seventy who knew, so she claimed, "all there was to know about children," even errant ones, and could govern them with a wise and effective hand. One day a boy whom they trusted and to whom they had given various privileges, suddenly disappeared. At the end of the afternoon he returned, with a bunch of live chickens in each hand. He explained that he had been troubled because "you ladies have such a hard time getting things for us." So he had gone to a place he knew of and fetched these chickens back for the Home. The greatest tact had to be used to explain to him that the chickens, so obviously stolen, must be returned; the Home could not conduct its business on that basis.

Sometimes it would be found that a child who seemed criminally inclined was really mentally disturbed and not responsible for his acts. A little boy with yellow curls and the face of a cherub managed to get hold of a can of kerosene. He poured some on the beds in the boys' dormitory and then set fire to them. All the boys could have run away in the tumult and confusion, but they did not. They turned to and put out the fire. It was Julia Lathrop who saw the need for psychiatric care for disturbed children and founded the first clinic for their needs.

One day the matron reported that the boys had been "acting badly"; in fact she had gone out to see what was going on and found that they had overpowered their guard. They had him on the floor, bound, and were jabbing him in the head with his own revolver. Mrs. Bowen asked whether she had not immediately sent for the police, but she declared, "Oh, no, that was not necessary." She told the boys to let the man get up and to apologize to him, which they did. She had no need of police. This was the only hint of an uprising that they ever had while this matron was at the Home.

In the end a special building was put up near Hull House for the Detention Home, a place of cleanliness and decent comfort, a place too of faith and affection and belief that these erring ones could learn to make something of themselves.

The Juvenile Court also had jurisdiction over dependent children, those no one wanted, those who had lost their parents or had been deserted by them. Their needs were not so difficult to meet, but there were occasions when curiously difficult situations arose. One of the judges once sent for Julia Lathrop in great haste; he declared that he was involved in a problem for which he could see no answer. She came at once.

A woman had adopted a little girl, apparently with her own mother's consent. The foster mother carried on a cheap and somewhat disreputable hotel, doing most of the work herself and toiling daily to the very edge of exhaustion. She felt it a matter of course that the little girl should do the same and by the time she was twelve the child was expected to take care of the horse — even poor families had to have a horse in those days since there was no other way to get about; to attend to the furnace and to wash great stacks of heavy dishes late every night. A woman who came to the hotel was so moved with pity for the child that, since she knew the foster mother would never give her up, she persuaded the little girl to run away with her to another county where, so she thought, the foster mother would not be able to get her back by law.

The foster mother, however, claiming that the child had been virtually abducted, had brought the matter into court. The judge was completely at a loss, since neither woman could qualify as a proper parent. He begged Julia Lathrop to be present at the hearing, and after the case had been presented, asked her if she would undertake to be the child's guardian and see that somehow she had a chance at a normal life. Julia had certainly not expected to adopt anyone, but she consented to take charge of her. The little girl put her hand confidently into Julia's and walked out with her. They left the judge with his own troubles, for he had told the two women that neither of them was fit to have custody of the child and each was expressing forcible indignation.

"Are you my mother now?" the little girl inquired of Miss Lathrop.

"No," Julia answered, "you have had enough mothers. The judge said that the state was going to take care of you. The governor asked me to do such things for the state."

"The state of Illinois has lots of towns in it, hasn't it?" the child asked. "So that I won't ever have to go back to where I stayed before?"

"Never so long as you live," was Julia's assurance.

Julia was responsible for the child for years afterward, until she was grown up and happily married, with children.

XI

An Assassination

The Presidential election of 1896 was held in the old
tradition of torchlight procession, bonfires and other picturesque trappings. For a long time afterward one could
come across in old attics and storage warehouses the white
oilcloth hats and capes which the marchers wore, and the
huge metal tubes which were the torches. They had mouth-
pieces on the side which, when blown into, made the flame
spout like a volcano. In the processions now and then one
could see a man being conveyed in a wheelbarrow, the result of some ridiculous bet, although it was difficult to
divine which had been the winner and which the loser.
These stimulating spectacles marked the political contest
between the calm and unexciting William McKinley and
the striking "silver-tongued orator" William Jennings
Bryan with his somewhat unstable and perhaps not too
widely understood doctrine of Free Silver. It was the latter
who, with Jane Addams, had been defeated in an inter-
collegiate debate so many years ago, the laurels going to
some obscure student who was never heard of again.

McKinley, duly elected, went steadily and steadfastly through a four-year term which included the difficult problems of the Spanish-American War, the intervention in Cuba and the annexing of the Philippines. So completely did he win the confidence of the American people that he was reelected in 1900 without any great opposition and without the fine fanfare which went out with William Jennings Bryan's first defeat. A somewhat reluctant Theodore Roosevelt found himself unexpectedly thrust into the position of Vice President.

The Buffalo Exposition, a minor-sized world's fair following the pattern of Chicago's more celebrated one, was opened in 1901. Since a President was always expected to lend his presence to such an undertaking, William McKinley went to Buffalo for that purpose. On September 6 he was present at a huge public reception, shaking hands with all comers when a man, Leon Czolgosz, approached, entirely unhampered by the supposed Secret Service guards. The fellow's hand was wrapped in a handkerchief. It covered a revolver, with which Czolgosz shot McKinley in the abdomen just as the President was reaching out to shake hands with him. Through eight stifling September days, with the whole country tense with excitement, and anxiety, the President lingered, then died on September 14, 1901.

The assassin was arrested at once. He admitted to being an anarchist, and at the very word a panic swept the country that matched only that when President Lincoln was shot and when the Haymarket bomb was thrown. It was a plot, people shrieked, an anarchist plot! The government was about to be seized by those long-feared anarchists! Terror ran everywhere. An order went out that everyone ever suspected of anarchy was to be seized and questioned.

The first victim in Chicago was a peaceable Russian Jew, Abraham Isaak, editor of a small anarchist paper. When it became known that he had once seen and talked to the assassin, he was arrested with his son and some associates and all of them were thrown — not into the ordinary city jail but, for fear of rescue attempts — into some long disused, filthy cells under the City Hall which were quite unfit for human habitation. His wife and daughter were taken to the police station for rigid questioning. The police would not allow Isaak or any of those with him to have access or communication to any friends; above all they were denied any legal counsel whatsoever, in spite of the fact that any accused or arrested person has the right to consult a lawyer.

Jane Addams had met the accused man two years before. A distinguished visitor from Russia, Prince Kropotkin, had come to the United States to lecture. He was a member of the Russian nobility who had, like Tolstoy, thrown in his lot with the lower classes suffering under the czarist government, but who had not been an advocate of violence in any way. He had been well received in America, he had spoken at the Universities of Illinois and Wisconsin and had been invited to speak before various literary and scientific societies in Chicago.

Prince Kropotkin had stayed at Hull House while he was in the neighborhood, and various of his compatriots had come to see him there, among them Abraham Isaak with his wife, his son and his daughter. Now the cry immediately arose that by allowing Isaak's visit, Hull House had aligned itself on the side of anarchy. Jane's unpopularity among some powerful groups of Chicago citizens had begun to wane a little, but it all broke out once more with this new fuel for the fire. Had she not stood up for the trade unions and their protests and requests? Had she not defended Governor Altgeld, who had pardoned the anarchists in prison? She might not be an anarchist herself, but she was certainly associated with them. All the sound and fury broke loose again. This man Isaak had once been received at Hull House. That was enough to suspect her of the worst.

Next day a small group of her neighbors, Russian Jews who lived near Hull House and with whom she was well acquainted, came to see her. Couldn't she, wouldn't she do something to help their countryman who was being held so close that no one could come to his aid? What was the use, they asked her bitterly, in talking of the law in America that protects everyone from illegal attack? They had come to believe in it, mainly through her teaching, but what could she say in defense of her country now?

It was one of her very difficult moments as she pondered upon what she ought to do. There was so much risk involved that her friends could not advise her; she had only herself to consult, herself and her profound belief. The daughter of John Addams did not hesitate long. With all other proper sources of help failing, the person to see in behalf of Isaak was the mayor. She would go to him immediately.

Mayor Carter Harrison had reason to know of all the good Jane Addams had done for Chicago through Hull House. He thought that she was "somewhat radical" but he was not blinded and deafened by the public clamor that could arise around her name. He was, however, careful of his own political reputation. He explained that the prisoners were being held "for their own protection" since there was fear that they might be lynched. He was very firm in refusing her request that they might see a lawyer. Before her protests he explained finally that he could not take the responsibility of letting the arrested persons see any of their associates, for fear it might provoke violence and also for fear of the imagined anarchist plot.

Yet if she herself was willing to assume the responsibility and the unfavorable publicity, he would be willing to let the accused persons consult with her as someone whom he felt to be above suspicion. It was plain that he was quite unwilling to provoke unfavorable publicity by interviewing them himself. Jane thought afterward that he might have been testing her, thinking she would decline the offer. But at the moment her only thought was that someone must bring aid to those so desperately in need of proper justice. She thanked the mayor. She would go at once.

Within half an hour she was in a dark and dismal prison corridor, surrounded by overbearing and hostile police. She talked to the shattered Isaak, who had heard nothing of his wife and daughter since the moment when they had been arrested along with him. She was able to reassure him; she had the mayor's promise that justice would be given him, and she departed, saying afterward that, "It did not seem very different from other interviews I have had with many another forlorn man who had fallen into prison," thus giving us a glimpse of some of her work which has no special record. She returned to Hull House to find it boiling with reporters, all disapproving and full of opprobrium, "traces of which, I suppose will always remain," she commented.

She was to receive a flood of abusive letters, some going far beyond decency in their expression, but she had a few that carried approbation, one from a federal judge whom she had never seen and one from a distinguished professor of constitutional law. Jane was so given to self-questioning that she found it difficult to be sure that she was right, but she took these few authoritative voices as reassuring and went on with her work undismayed. It seemed that her stock had fallen as low as it could ever get, yet later it would go lower yet.

With the lack of reasonableness that is characteristic of suddenly aroused public opinion, none of her detractors took much notice of the fact that when tried at last, no real evidence could ever be found against Abraham Isaak. He and his companions were presently set free, fully exonerated. Governor Altgeld, in his report on the Haymarket trials, had made it clear for all time that packed juries and unfair judgments were not to be allowed to pass unnoticed, and these men did get a fair trial.

Czolgosz was tried and executed without any very great publicity. He was obviously of unsound mind but not enough so to save him from the death penalty. He had admitted that "a lecture on anarchy" had given him the stimulus to plot the crime, and that was enough to condemn him. It was the only part that anarchy had played in the tragic affair.

One small touching incident came to Jane's notice before the story was entirely ended. She came across a German cobbler, desperately poor but preferring to have his own shop and work by hand rather than take part in the modern methods of producing shoes. The man said he had been an anarchist once, but with the years his feeling toward their ideas had slipped into the mildness of old age. Czolgosz, who was very young, had come to see him only a few days before the crime, on his way to Buffalo. He wanted, so he said, to know what "the password" was, thinking that there was an anarchist's sign to be exchanged among comrades. There was no password. He had asked others for it, and been told that such a thing did not exist. The German shoemaker told him the same thing and the young man had gone away with few more words.

"If I had only known," the cobbler said. "If I had only known!"

He told Jane that in his own fiery youth in Germany he had been convinced that the Church as well as the State was oppressing human society and he had made up his mind that the murder of some important political or religious official would be a spectacular and effectual protest. For a year he had carried a concealed weapon, turning over and over in his mind the plans for his dark purpose. Then one day, in a burst of confidence, he told his whole idea and intention to a close friend, and in the telling suddenly realized how empty and fatuous the scheme was.

"That poor fellow just sat beside me on my bench; if I had put my hand on his shoulder and said, 'Now look here, brother, what is on your mind? . . . Tell me, I have seen much of life and understand all kinds of men. I have been young and hotheaded and foolish myself!' " — the poor old man felt that if he could have persuaded Czolgosz to speak of what he was about to do, his purpose might have crumbled and "The whole nation might have been spared this horror." The old shoemaker could not forgive himself for what he had not done.

The next year John Altgeld died. Fifty thousand persons

passed by his coffin to pay their last respects as he lay in state in the Chicago Public Library. These were the humble people whom he had benefited. But his enemies were still powerful. Only three people dared to speak in eulogy at his funeral. One was the minister Dr. Frank Crane, one was his law partner, Clarence Darrow. The third was Jane Addams. Even those around her at Hull House urged her against it. This would be the last straw in the weight of public opinion.

"If you do this, Hull House will lose all its influence," they urged — to say nothing of its financial support, of which a great deal had already been withdrawn. But it did not deter her, and she spoke fearlessly in praise of a great man.

In regard to the withdrawals of support she maintained not only a tolerant but a humorous spirit. She speaks in her memoirs of how "we were entertained" by the statement of one rich woman who canceled her contribution to Hull House because, traveling abroad recently, she had met various members of the Russian aristocracy, who told her that the revolutionary feeling in Russia was entirely uncalled for and unnecessary. This was apropos of the support Hull House was giving to a notable Russian revolutionary refugee. It was before the Bolsheviks had taken over the revolution. In time the United States would be the haven for a vast number of similar political fugitives.

It was a more serious matter when Mrs. Potter Palmer withdrew her support. She was the most prominent woman in Chicago society, its leader and arbiter. Her entertainments were fabulous and her invitations greatly coveted. It is a legend, which should probably be taken with the grain of salt that goes with all legends, that once in the midst of one of these enormous entertainments a guest got lost in the vast house and presently found herself facing the back stairs — with Potter Palmer himself sitting on them, waiting until the party should be over. The architect who had given him this fabulous medieval castle on the Lake Shore had neglected to provide a place of refuge for the master of the house. But Mrs. Potter Palmer aided Hull House no more.

It may be thought, from the way Jane Addams unflinchingly faced her unpopularity, and her refusal to let it influence her decisions, that in time she had become indifferent to it. That was not true. She continued to suffer deeply from the steadily mounting criticism, and to be aware of how much it actually did rob her work of its support. How uncertain she could be that she was right when all hands were against her! But in loyalty to a friend, to someone who had her same ideals and was willing to suffer for them, she would not falter. Although she could not yet be aware of it, she was soon to have a champion, an unquestioning supporter of high station, the President of the United States.

Before he was governor of New York, Theodore Roosevelt made his first mark in politics by reorganizing and reforming New York City's notoriously corrupt police force. While he was governor he interested himself in slum clearance and came across the record of what Jane Addams and Hull House had been doing in exploring, investigating, and so far as it could be done at that time, in relieving the evil conditions under which poor people were living.

She had by then had her tilt with Johnny Power, and was at that time being spoken of as "one of Chicago's foremost citizens." Roosevelt fell into the habit of stopping at Hull House whenever he was in the city and discussing politics and reform needs with her. He was present at a review of Boy Scouts on one occasion and saw a play acted by the Hull House Players — *Justice*, by John Galsworthy, its first presentation in the United States. He was unacquainted with Galsworthy, and being a voracious reader, he gathered as many of Galsworthy's books as he could find and carried them away to read on the train.

After the Boy Scout review he had gone with Jane to address a large audience of immigrants who had just received their papers for American citizenship. On the way he asked her how long she had been a suffragist. The rising tide of the movement for votes for women was all about them now. Jane had first been introduced to it at Rockford Seminary, which was boiling with it in her day. Her father had been convinced of the rightness of women's having a vote and, so she told Mr. Roosevelt, it was he who had taught her the worth of women's suffrage.

There were good arguments both against and for it. Roosevelt observed in reply, "You are one of the best of these arguments in yourself." She thanked him and later listened to his stirring speech to the immigrants at the Second Regiment Armory in which he announced firmly that he had always believed that women should have the vote. It is possible that he had asked the question merely to test her; it scarcely seems probable that, good argument as she was for women's suffrage, she could have converted him on that brief drive from Hull House to the Armory. His steadily expressed opinion that votes for women were merely "simple justice" could hardly have been born in that moment, but it convinced many doubters of the time.

Later that same day, as he and Jane drove through an immense throng to lunch at the Union League Club, Jane's hat blew away and vanished in the crowd. T.R. insisted on taking off his own tall silk hat and rode bareheaded beside her. The Union League sent Jane a check for fifty dollars for a new one. She returned it saying that the hat had only cost ten dollars when it was new and was now two years old.

Theodore Roosevelt, coming into office at McKinley's death, was to cut a broad swath across the history of his time. He began at once. The London *Punch's* great cartoonist Bernard Partridge represented the American eagle in a washtub, very wet and bedraggled, being violently scrubbed by a delightedly grinning T.R.

The work of Hull House was now to reach farther afield and join forces with a staunch ally. Florence Kelley had not been available to take part in the efforts to set up and maintain the Chicago Juvenile Court through its first troubled years. The Consumers' League, of which she was now made executive secretary, had been founded in 1891 by a working girl, Alice Woodbridge, backed by Mrs. Josephine Shaw Lowell. Miss Woodbridge had also founded the New York Charity Organization Society, which undertook to organize the efforts of private charity effectively for combined action against poverty and depression.

The Consumers' League set out to use the buying power of the public to emphasize the protests against long hours, low wages and unjust treatment of the youthful workers. People who joined pledged themselves to refuse to buy anything which did not have the Consumers' League white label, guaranteeing that the product had been made in a factory where fair working conditions and employment practices existed. It was not a very large organization but it managed to be singularly powerful, and when it entered on a drive with other supporters, it went far toward achieving laws for the protection and better treatment of workers, especially working women and children.

Under Florence Kelley's direction the Consumers' League gathered facts about industrial conditions and made reports on them to the public. They helped to picket in the case of the great shirtwaist strike, where young girls were arrested and imprisoned in the same cells with abandoned women criminals. Their main program was to help get legal redress when wages were below the ordinary cost of living and to achieve a minimum-hours law for women which would recognize the fact that they could not and should not endure the same working hours as men. It can well be imagined that the advent of Florence Kelley brought great activity and influence to the organization. Through her move to New York and her residence at the Henry Street Settlement headed by Lillian Wald, Hull House became more closely connected with the work that was going on under different leaders in other places toward the same end.

Jane Addams was the first to make it clear, through the Hull House investigations and reports, how vast was the work to be done and what effort would be needed to make any impression on the growing industrial inequality. By 1893, settlements were coming into being on various sides, the Henry Street House and Greenwich House in New York, the Chicago Commons, and others. Henceforth Hull House was to have allies for social betterment in greater and greater numbers. The force emanating from these numerous organizations was beginning to be felt all across the country.

There was great demand upon Jane for speaking engagements, which she filled whenever she could manage the time, and it seems miraculous how much she was able to do, with addresses at various colleges and universities besides the Chicago University extension courses. Magazines asked her for articles, and in time publishers were suggesting books, since she was showing herself to be as forcible and convincing a writer as a speaker.

Out of the growing number of residents at Hull House, many besides Julia Lathrop and Florence Kelley were to become leaders in other social organizations, with their own large accomplishments. There was Mary McDowell of the Chicago Stock Yards Settlement; there were the two Abbotts, Grace and Edith, each to be head of a notable enterprise. There was Frances Perkins, Franklin Roosevelt's Secretary of Labor. Each had the privilege of knowing Jane Addams well, each was inspired by her. Each of them, for the most part with the backing of their families, contributed freely to the enterprise which was accomplishing so much. At a memorial service in honor of Mary Rozet Smith's mother, Sarah Rozet Smith, Jane Addams said that in addition to her other generosities "she gave graciously to Hull House that most precious gift — the time and services of her daughter." Jane's father would certainly have given her as graciously to the work on which she had set her heart.

Hull House's efforts toward needed reform, and those of the workers who went out from Hull House, were bringing in an increasing fund of experience and information. There was now a growing body of trained social workers; there was also the Consumers' League; there were charitable organizations working in the light of wider knowledge of real

conditions and more deeply comprehended needs. Schools
for social workers steadily multiplied.

Florence Kelley, in her vigorous administration of the
Consumers' League, had set up in New York various projects of direct fact-gathering. A young friend of hers, Carola
Woerishoffer, who had made a brilliant record in her
studies of politics and economics at Bryn Mawr College,
had presented herself at Greenwich House, another successful settlement in New York, to say, "I have come to
help and to learn." She was quickly set to work on gathering information for Florence Kelley's reports.

Certain labor agencies in New York were exploiting the
inexperienced immigrants who were flocking in from Europe. It was easy to take advantage of their ignorance and
persuade them, immediately on arrival, to accept disad-
vantageous contracts from which they could not easily
escape. Carola Woerishoffer would pass herself off as a
newly arrived immigrant girl, find out the real nature of the
employment offered, and bring its unfairness to light. She
chose particularly work in laundries, and since she was
often fired for resistance to unfair treatment by tyrannical
foremen, her experience became wide. Her reports were as
brief and forcible as Florence Kelley's own.

She was eventually employed by the City of New York's
Labor Commission to inspect the contractors' camps for
immigrant workmen which were scattered about outside
Manhattan. She carried out her duties effectively, going
from place to place in her own car. It was in the fairly early
days of automobiles, the roads were bad, the hazards many.
On a day in September 1911, her car went over an embank-
ment. Her companion from Greenwich House was unhurt,

but Carola was crushed under the steering wheel, and on the next day died of her injuries.

She was a young woman of large means in her own right, and she had left a very substantial sum to her college. Under the planning of President Carey Thomas, Bryn Mawr proceeded to establish in her memory a graduate school for the training of social workers, the Carola Woerishoffer Graduate Department of Social Economy and Social Research. It was the first of its kind in the country to recognize the need for social research on a scholarly basis and to have the resources and support of a college faculty behind it. Other schools for social workers had tended to avoid too close an official connection with universities or colleges, believing that academic trends of thought might be too theoretical to be joined with practical activities. But the recognition of the need for extended and organized research was so plainly a step forward that the other schools rapidly followed suit. It is an accepted stipulation today that an accredited school for social training must be allied with an established university or college.

While criticism of Jane Addams waxed and waned in Chicago, her real friends never failed to stand by her. They had become a large and distinguished group, all of them well aware of what was being accomplished in social history under her leadership. In the philosophy department at the University of Chicago young Doctor Dewey was rapidly coming to be considered one of the important thinkers of his time. His revolutionary theories concerning education were undergoing experimentation in a school for children sponsored by the university. Conservative people at first made fun of his ideas as wildly impractical, but there are few now who do not realize how completely they have altered teaching methods for the better. It is easy to see why, with their vigorous beliefs, he and Jane Addams were such friends, why he came often to Hull House to lecture to the Plato Club of argumentative old men and to the younger groups gathered there.

Others of Jane's firm supporters were Professor Albion Small, who established the first sociology department at the University of Chicago, and Dr. Grahame Taylor, who had founded the Chicago Commons. It is clear in their surviving letters to Jane how much they admired her, partook of her ideas and looked to her leadership. She did not keep copies of her own letters; only those have survived which Mary Rozet Smith treasured through their whole friendship and which have given us such a rich insight into what Jane Addams was and what she was doing.

Although the circle immediately about Jane lost Florence Kelley in 1900, it received at almost the same time an addition in the person of very young, very sincere and eminently able and likable Dr. Alice Hamilton. In her autobiography, *Exploring the Dangerous Trades*, Alice Hamilton gives us a clearly etched view of Hull House in the early twentieth century. She had once heard Jane Addams deliver a public lecture in the Methodist Church of her home town. She came away convinced and enthusiastic, and through the intervening years of her study of medicine she had kept her heart set on becoming a resident at Hull House as soon as circumstances made it possible.

The first night that Alice Hamilton had dinner in the big Hull House dining room had been a gala occasion. Governor Altgeld was that evening a guest of honor. It was after his defeat for reelection and this was Hull House's gesture of continuing support. All the residents ate to-

Alice Hamilton

gether, so Alice was able to hear the conversation at the main table where Julia Lathrop and Florence Kelley were telling the former governor some of their experiences as inspectors. Some of their adventures were dramatic, some moving, some absurd. Vivid scenes and humorous situations alike were brilliantly described. If the two women chanced to be on opposite sides of an argument, sparks would fly, and no one would dare to take part in a conversation in which the level of exchange was so rapid and so incisive. The pair of friends differed often, for Florence Kelley would take no person's opinion unchallenged. But no hard feeling ever came out of these arguments.

Alice Hamilton herself was blond, slim, graceful, good-looking, and very shy. In that friendly atmosphere she was a contrast as different as night from day from Florence Kelley. Their residences at Hull House overlapped briefly, giving Alice Hamilton opportunity first to be afraid of Mrs. Kelley's merciless tongue, but almost immediately after to admire and love her. After leaving Chicago, Mrs. Kelley never failed to report at Hull House whenever she passed through on her speaking tours for the Consumers' League. On such occasions the long halls and high-ceilinged rooms rang with laughter and good talk.

XII

The Triangle Company Fire

Various manufacturing companies in New York carried on their operations in old loft buildings which everyone knew were veritable firetraps. The Triangle Shirt Company was one of many running the risk of disaster without thought of anything but the profits.

Their building had fire escapes as the law required, but the rooms opening on them were kept locked because there had been some petty thievery. A lighted cigarette, discarded by a careless workman, started a blaze that spread instantly through the old dry walls and floors, making a roaring furnace of the whole interior. Staircases and elevator shafts at once became flaming chimneys. A hundred and forty-three workers, almost all young women, lost their lives by burning or by jumping to their death in the street below. The firemen's ladders were not tall enough to reach the high windows. Nets were held to catch those who jumped, but the momentum of those falling bodies was so great that it jerked the firemen off their feet. The people watching in the street could see a young man helping the

THE TRIANGLE COMPANY FIRE

girls over the windowsill, persuading them to jump either as a shred of hope, or as the less painful death. They saw him kiss his fiancée goodbye before she jumped. Neither survived.

Public feeling expressed itself in a great mass meeting a few days later at the Metropolitan Opera House. Hundreds were there to protest their horror at a tragedy that could have been so easily prevented, and to search for measures which would insure that it could never happen again. It was revealed that the workers for the Triangle Shirt Company had tried to organize a union to press for better and safer conditions, but had been refused. A representative of labor, a young cap maker who had organized a union in another company, was asked to speak. She stood, small but completely undaunted, at the edge of the great stage, with her voice reaching to every quarter of the vast audience.

She did not attempt to blame the factory owners, responsible for the disaster, nor the fire inspectors whose carelessness has let such unspeakable hazards go unchecked. But she bitterly denounced society itself for permitting a system that held human life so cheap.

The result of the meeting was the passage of a New York law for the Factory Investigating Committee. A former resident of Hull House and graduate of the New York School of Philanthropy, Frances Perkins, was chosen by the governor to be the head of it. She had stood in the street to watch the Triangle fire herself.

As the new sense of responsibility spread through public opinion, Jane Addams's leadership began to be felt more and more. She had always been a convincing public speaker, as William Kent, giver of the Hull House playground, and many others could testify. It was now becoming apparent that she was an equally convincing and moving writer. A succession of books by her, published in the course of ten years, made this fact evident.

In the first one, a small volume entitled *Democracy and Social Ethics,* she drew on her experiences and observations during the Pullman strikes, the political struggle against John Power, and from the course of her day-to-day living as a member of the Hull House neighborhood. The title seemed rather forbidding — she always said she was not good at composing titles — but the contents make lively human reading, since all her theories are illustrated by incidents out of her personal experience. She speaks with feeling of the situation of young women who come to maturity with the desire to be of service to society, yet are held back by the narrow prejudice of their elders.

In another chapter she gives very definite directions for the method of approach a social visitor should use in an interview with a person to whom she hopes to give effective aid. By all means the client's dignity (the word "case" is steadily avoided) is not to be assailed by any hint of patronage nor any invasion of his privacy. The separate chapters had originally been a series of lectures which she had given at various times and places. She offered them in a book as a possible basis for the procedure to be followed by a completely inexperienced and probably somewhat embarrassed social visitor.

Other books and articles were published in the early years of the century. *Newer Ideals of Peace* came out in 1907, to bring her praise in a few quarters but, in many the same sort of blame that the militant T.R. had given her after reading it. Meanwhile, she was planning and writing the book which was to be the embodiment of her deepest beliefs. She called it *The Spirit of Youth and the City Streets*. Published in 1909, it contains all the wisdom distilled from her experience in helping a young generation understand the old, and the older one to find tolerance of youth. To arm herself for that struggle, she had made for years every effort to understand youth on her own part, to discover its needs and to meet them, to comprehend its misunderstandings and to correct them, along with the misunderstandings of parents, teachers, and representatives of the law. How much, how very much, of the whole organization of Hull House had been devoted to that single purpose! To society at large, Jane was declaring that it held the mandate for the welfare of burgeoning generations and yet was ignoring its responsibilities and opportunities. As a result, young people were in peril of losing their most valued possessions: their enthusiasms, their ingenuousness, their innocence and hope.

She knew, and voiced her knowledge now, that children and young people all need the same fundamental things, that besides shelter and food and education they must have opportunities for the enlargement of spirit and imagination, that when their working years begin they need, indeed are starved for, some change and relaxation. She knew further that coming to marriageable age, boys and girls alike need some chance to know each other, some opportunity for natural acquaintance, so that they do not enter on married life precipitately with some hastily chosen stranger. Young boys playing in the city streets, as boys must play to give vent to exuberant spirits, were so constantly interrupted by traffic or policemen that there was no continuity or chance for imagination in their games. Girls did not even have the street for a playground. They could only play on the much-trodden tenement steps.

In a foreword to *The Spirit of Youth and the City Streets*, Jane Addams hoped that it might "prove of value to those groups of people who, in many cities, are making a gallant effort to minimize the dangers which surround young people." It has been not only of value but of true inspiration. Its greatness — for it is a great book — lies in the fact that it voices the real depth of a great woman's conviction.

The years were passing; it was 1909 and Hull House was twenty years old. Jane embarked on a history of those truly momentous years. She had actually acquired a secretary by this time, and the two had developed a unique method of work, appropriate to an author immensely busy and in demand, and to a secretary untiringly willing to turn her hand to a thousand other matters in which she might be of service. They acquired a large roll of paper of the proper width to go into the typewriter and Jane would dictate whenever the busy day afforded a moment, the recollections her mind had been gathering. No attempt was made to present them in any succession in time, they just came out, as matters worth recording kept occurring to her. Later this long sheet would be cut apart and consecutive incidents joined together to form a continuous narrative. It was published under the title *Twenty Years at Hull House*.

To make things clear she gave some passages of autobiography, from which we get insight into her childhood in the little town in Illinois and into her soul-searching during those intervening years, and finally her finding of Hull House. The rest of the account is an enchantingly personal

Jane Addams at her desk in 1910

and frank record of the persons, the problems, the errors and the accomplishments of that adventurous project.

Among the many criticisms that prejudiced people found to cast at Hull House was the statement that no religious services were offered there. The inference was that Jane was not a religiously minded person. This was not true. Like her father, she was something of a nonconformist, but like him she thoroughly respected and honored the beliefs of others. After she came to live at Hull House she officially joined the little, struggling Congregational church which was close by. For a period it had a minister who was a very earnest young person, very intolerant, and greatly lacking in judgment concerning human character. Jane found his sermons so contrary to her own beliefs and to her faith in the value and goodness of the world of people about her that she did not attend services during the latter part of his stay. He, in his zeal, managed to persuade his congregation to drop Miss Addams from membership. After his departure, the church saw its error and wished to restore her to their fellowship. There could be no mistaking, either then or now, that strong Christian spirit which made Hull House such an astounding success. Jane Addams accepted both incidents without rancor. She did not speak of the matter in her book, but at the end of it she did explain one important point. After experimenting with the bewildering number of faiths represented by those who flocked to the doors of Hull House, "we found unsatisfactory the diluted form of worship which we could carry on together."

Alice Hamilton had become a strong pillar of the work which Miss Addams was recording. Jane had always liked, if possible, to have a doctor among her residents; they had come and gone as circumstances brought or removed them. But Alice Hamilton was concentrating her whole interest and purpose upon Jane and Hull House. Her close connection with it and with Jane herself was to last as long as Jane lived. Besides her outside work which was her means of support, Miss Hamilton conducted a "well babies clinic," saying that she was not yet expert enough to pronounce on sick babies, but could advise their mothers or give warnings when some further examination was necessary.

Hull House had a row of baths available to the public. Here on Saturdays Dr. Hamilton held a well-attended baby-bathing ceremony. Later she urged Hull House to suggest that the city government should establish public baths in larger numbers than Hull House could afford. The reply of the authorities at first was that poor people did not bathe. Under pressure, however, city baths were finally established and were constantly and eagerly in demand.

By sheer necessity, Alice Hamilton's shyness was rapidly

worn away in the lighthearted group of the Hull House residents. They divided themselves into the Old Guard and the Young Guard; there were also classifications of the Noble Set and the Frivolous Set. When one reads Alice Hamilton's *Autobiography*, one might be tempted to class her as one of the Frivolous Set, since she writes with such pleasure of the Sunday walking excursions into the sand dunes, Chicago's hinterland, of the bicycle trips, the gay visits to the Yiddish theater, the one good playhouse in the neighborhood, or to the absurd melodramatic offerings of the smaller places of dramatic entertainment. Florence Kelley's son, whom they called Ko, was now grown to an age to be a part of these cheery adventures. All of it was in the atmosphere of warmhearted and congenial good company.

There was, however, nothing of frivolity in the work that Alice Hamilton was doing at Hull House. Even as she grew to be at home there, she had a pair of terrors which she could not put behind her. She was afraid of reporters and policemen. She went through an ugly but illuminating experience which showed clearly what the attitude of the newspapers of Chicago was toward Hull House at that time. It was shortly after the Averbuch incident, when the young Russian was shot, on a mistaken impulse, by the Chicago chief of police. A reporter from one of the city's newspapers arrived at Hull House announcing that he must see Miss Addams.

Ordinarily Julia Lathrop saw such visitors and knew by experience just how to deal with them. Unfortunately she was away, and Alice Hamilton had not yet acquired the necessary technique. Jane was upstairs, ill with tonsilitis, so Dr. Hamilton told the journalist that he could not be received. He refused to go away, however, and pushed his way upstairs and into Miss Addams's room.

Was it not true, he demanded, that this anarchist Averbuch was a visitor received at Hull House?

Jane replied that it was not true. The boy had been learning English at another settlement but had never been in Hull House.

The representative of the press held his ground. "I may as well tell you, Miss Addams," he said, "that I have orders from my paper to connect Averbuch with Hull House and I am going to do it."

Such tactics were familiar enough to Jane Addams. She never made any effort at public denial; it only aroused controversy, she said, and called undue attention to statements that were manifest lies. But Alice Hamilton did not find the occasion very reassuring in respect to her fear of reporters.

At another difficult time she did better. She was coming back too Hull House one day and saw a group of men, all Russians, having an argument on the street corner over the respective merits of Mensheviks and Bolsheviks. Voices had been raised, fists were being shaken, heavy boots stamped the pavement. She saw that a gathering of policemen were standing at a little distance, evidently deciding whether or not this was disorderly conduct which called for them to step in and make arrests.

Dr. Hamilton managed to make herself go up to the principal officer and explain, "These men are not fighting. They are only arguing over politics. This is the way they do it."

"Lady," he replied, "you people oughtn't to let these

people come here. If I had my way they'd all be lined up against a wall and shot."

This far from quieting statement impelled her to wait in tense anxiety for an hour while the argument went on, until it melted suddenly and came to a wholly peaceable end.

During the visits young Dr. Hamilton made in the neighborhood of Hull House she began to come across increasing evidence of the various illnesses arising from uninspected working conditions. She found cases of a specially vicious form of lead poisoning among a number of employees of the Pullman Company. Of these she made official complaint, but with little effect.

Louise Bowen, who had already given so much service to Hull House and its neighbors, now joined her efforts to Alice Hamilton's. She was a wealthy woman, and among other things owned a large block of Pullman stock. She made energetic demands that this matter of lead poisoning should be investigated and eradicated, and was met by the board of directors with stubborn resistance. As she came before them again and again, one of the directors asked her why she did not sell her stock and break all connection with the company if she did not like the methods of the management. Her stouthearted reply was that she had no intention of selling her stock but would continue her complaints until the bad conditions were remedied. This she proceeded to do, with eventual success.

The background of social conditions was changing with the larger number of workers now in the field. Jane Addams's name was an important one everywhere and she was beginning to have some strong allies. One of them in particular was Lillian Wald in New York, the friend and supporter of Florence Kelley, who lived with her on Henry Street. Miss Wald was a younger woman with gifts and ideals somewhat similar to Jane's, but with a different approach and a different personality. Like Jane, and like the imaginary young woman of whom Jane speaks in *Democracy and Social Ethics*, on growing up she found herself possessed of education, money, and a firm intention to make her life of some use to others, but with not much knowledge of how to begin.

Miss Wald was a person of quite notable beauty, of gracious and appealing charm. She had, moreover, a large measure of solid common sense and executive ability. She took a course in nursing, with much the same idea that Jane had had when she set out to study medicine as a means of getting close to people who needed her. Besides her nursing study, she undertook to teach a class of women from the poorer part of New York who aspired to be nurses also, but who had too little education to qualify them for nursing school. It chanced that one of her students was ill and sent her little boy to notify her. Lillian went back with him to see her, in the shabby tenement and squalid surroundings where she was forced to live. The sight of such need, such utter deprivation of all the comforts, even the necessities of decent living, so struck the sheltered soul of Lillian Wald that she then and there knew what was to be her vocation — to live among people like these and to try, by sharing their kind of life, to show them how to make their lot a little better. Nursing would open the door to that accomplishment.

With a friend she found lodgings in a tenement on New York's East Side, made them comfortable and habitable at small expense, and set up an organized visiting nurse service, small at first and something completely new. The two friends soon moved into larger quarters on Henry Street, and increased their number as they could get sufficient funds. They did not call the place a settlement in the beginning, just "the House on Henry Street." But the nursing service brought them at once close to the lives of the people whom they attended. The necessity of learning to know and understand them in order to help them brought the nurses into the activities which a settlement inevitably takes on, and they became the Henry Street Settlement.

Lillian Wald and Jane Addams had become acquainted by 1898. A letter from Miss Wald exists which speaks of a visit Jane Addams made to Henry Street, and what deep inspiration Lillian Wald had drawn from it. The two moved quickly into close friendship and complete understanding of one another. Mrs. Kelley was a go-between for them as she went back and forth in her travels. Many ideas which began at one place or the other were discussed, shaped and developed at both ends of the line of communications. Such discussions partook of Lillian Wald's creative thought, Florence Kelley's vigorous advocacy, Julia Lathrop's tact and executive skill and Jane Addams's clear and steady wisdom. Lillian Wald invariably spoke of Jane Addams with deep affectionate admiration. "She is the leader of us all," she always acknowledged.

The fearful lesson of the Triangle Company fire gave impetus to the progress of social measures through the years that followed. All the long effort that had gone before, all the disappointments met and faced with unquenched hope and untiring effort were having their effect. Those were very fruitful years, and much was to be accomplished before the fateful assassinations at Sarajevo ushered in the First World War and turned all effort elsewhere. One of the largest projects of that propitious time was the establishment of the nationally sponsored Children's Bureau.

XIII

The Children's Bureau

Many ideas were first discussed at Hull House, and shaped and tested by the brilliant group that lived and worked there. These ideas were to develop and probably pass through other hands and minds before coming to ultimate fulfillment. To trace the growth of the concept of the Children's Bureau we must pursue it from its inception at Hull House in Chicago, through its proposal to colleagues by Lillian Wald in New York, past a special conference at the White House where many voices agreed to advocate it. It was finally framed and given substance by Congress in a measure passed by that body in April 1912 and signed into law by President Taft immediately after.

One of the early records of Hull House activities was a small book, mostly sponsored by Julia Lathrop, called *Hull House Maps and Papers*, published in 1896. It described the different nationalities of immigrants living in the neighborhood, indicated some of the problems for which the settlement was seeking a solution, and emphasized certain things that should be accomplished. It contained a characteristically vigorous article by Florence Kelley which included this novel suggestion: a special United States Commission for Children should be set up which would be devoted entirely to study of their development and welfare. It may be quite certain that before the suggestion was allowed to go into print the idea had been thoroughly discussed by the able minds at Hull House. But it was to lie fallow for a number of years. The time was not yet ripe for it.

Florence Kelley had carried the idea with her when she moved to New York and had talked it over with Lillian Wald at Henry Street. On a morning in 1903 these two women sat together at breakfast at the Henry Street Settlement with the morning paper between them. Lillian Wald seized on one item. It spoke of a plan for the Department of Agriculture to make a special study of the cotton-boll weevil which was threatening southern crops. If the government could set up a special bureau for this investigation, she commented, they could surely have a special organization that would support the care and welfare of children. The two friends talked over the matter, and a little later Miss Wald passed the idea on to Dr. Edward T. Devine, a professor of sociology at Columbia and general secretary of the New York Charity Organization Society. He was a person given to active measures and one who knew what the best approaches were. He sent a telegram to President Theodore Roosevelt, outlining the plan and asking for its approval. T.R. responded at once that it was "a bully idea, come down and tell me about it."

Lillian Wald went with Dr. Devine. Their interview with the President resulted in the first of a most important series of steps for the well-being of all children. In 1909 the first White House conference on the care of dependent children was called. It was attended by a number of important social leaders, Jane Addams among them. The conference passed a resolution recommending to Congress a bill establishing a Federal Children's Bureau "to investigate and report on matters relating to children's welfare," and stating also that "In our judgment the establishment of such a bureau is desirable."

T.R. cooperated with energy and promptness by sending a special message to Congress urging that such a bill be passed. That body immediately began committee hearings concerning the enactment of such a law. "The lack of it is discreditable to us as a people," the President stated with true T.R. vigor, "and in the absence [of such research] many abuses have gone unchecked." A number of persons attending the conference stayed on in Washington to speak before the congressional committee to explain the bill and the urgent necessity of its passage.

There was resistance to the enactment of the law through an attempt to show that such a bureau would merely duplicate work done by existing committees and commissions in different departments of the government. The real resistance, thus slightly disguised, was from those familiar forces of industry that suspected in the measure a possible threat to child labor, a well-justified misgiving as time was to show.

The National Child Labor Committee had also been sponsoring the idea of a children's bureau ever since its early proposal by Florence Kelley. In 1912 Julia Lathrop had spoken of it movingly before the National Conference of Charities and Corrections. "Pity . . . is the Kingdom of Heaven working within us. The justice of today is born of yesterday's pity. . . . This bureau is an expression of the nation's sense of justice." In all of the brilliant career of the convincing Julia Lathrop, this speech may have been her most significant and her best.

Argument for and against the bill dragged on. T.R. went out of office and William Howard Taft came in. The bill was finally presented to the Senate in 1912 by the redoubtable Senator Borah, so well known for his influence and his progressive ideas that his colleagues called him the One-Man Party. It was passed by both Houses and President Taft signed it into law.

The bill had specified that the director of the new bureau was to be nominated by the President, and presented to the Senate "to advise and consent." Taft's choice was Julia Lathrop. There would go with Julia, besides her own compelling personality, all that she had learned at Hull House. On account of the congressional hearings, in which she had taken lively and effective part, she was already a familiar figure to many of the senators. There was no hesitation in the vote to affirm her appointment.

The bill providing for the Children's Bureau was accompanied by only a small appropriation, nor was it a permanent one, but had to be renewed every year. The staff must necessarily be small. It was a difficult matter to decide just what project to adopt first. What aspect of the large needs ought to be studied before any other? Julia Lathrop did not hesitate — she chose babies.

Her experience with them had possibly begun with that little fellow whom she and Jane Addams had unexpectedly ushered into the world without professional assistance. She knew more now and also was aware of how much more ought to be known. She set about gathering material for a report of facts and information for mothers which was to be published as soon as possible.

A full investigation of the conditions which were to be the subject of this first report on the lives and welfare of American mothers and babies called for widespread research everywhere — literally everywhere. Julia Lathrop had learned all about the technique of such research during the time that she was investigator for the state of Illinois. She could instruct her helpers now in the very complex task of learning in their own turn just how people lived. Information was to be assembled among prosperous people and, more important, among the great multitudes of the needy. It meant the traversing of miles of city streets, the climbing of many steep tenement stairs to knock at sagging doors.

The survey was caried out in nine representative cities. Many of the women who made these preliminary investigations were volunteers working under committees of the General Federation of Women's Clubs, all of them glad and eager to be of help to Miss Lathrop and the new agency for children. An expert on statistics had been added to the bureau's staff, to sift the facts and figures gathered and prepare for the reading of their real meaning and possible implication. All the work being done was in a new field. The assembling of the facts was not to be a mere sampling of the situation in a certain group or a small area. A whole community was to be covered, all the mothers questioned and the babies examined, with records made of births, of deaths, and of illnesses up to twelve months old.

As the first-chosen member of the new organization, Julia Lathrop had invited a fellow resident of Hull House to be the medical representative. She was Grace Meigs, that same young doctor who had once blundered at midnight into the spacious marble-paved foyer of the old hotel-turned-tenement of Chicago's formerly fashionable West Side. She was to write this first report, and to do it under pressure for time, since it was not only badly needed but it must show at once what sort of thing the new bureau was setting out to do.

Dr. Meigs worked long and arduously to meet the deadline. The day came when the last pages were to be finished and that night the weary author struggled on in a silent office while the sound of footsteps outside diminished and died away, while the roar of traffic ceased for that brief interval between full darkness and dawn. Washington is a magically beautiful city in the early morning. It has little smoke and the clear light touches the white buildings one after another with the faint colors of dawn. By full daylight the task was done.

The report came out and gave rise at once to two pamphlets for the instruction of parents, *Prenatal Care* issued in 1913 and *Infant Care* a year later. A fellow worker in the bureau said later of Dr. Meigs and her long labor, "There are hundreds of babies living today because of her." It was also because of the bureau itself, its director and consultant committee and all those who had toiled to collect the facts that betrayed America's indifference to its children. The two publications were distributed in hundreds, then they began to be asked for in thousands, especially *Infant Care*. Congressmen sent in requests for quantities of them to pass on to their constituents and a special service was set up to supply their needs.

Dr. Meigs's report brought to light some startling and unwelcome truths. The death rate of babies and mothers at birth in the United States — in clean, sanitary, well-

equipped America — was definitely higher than in many of
the less well-endowed countries. It was almost the highest
in the world. It showed further that the death rate of
babies went up as their fathers' wage rates went down.
Children fared less well on bottles than when their
mothers could nurse them. Children who were cared for at
home by mothers who were not working did better than
children in institutions no matter how well managed. An
examination into the causes of the deaths of mothers and
babies showed that the largest number of these deaths were
preventable if sufficient care was given the mother before
the baby was born.

The Children's Bureau next produced a movie to il-
lustrate the proper methods of bathing, dressing and feeding a small child. Julia Lathrop and her medical colleague
decided that the substance of it, while very useful, was
rather dull and should be enlivened. So they added an
extra character besides the young mother and the instruct-
ing nurse. They searched the attic of some friends and
produced a costume slightly earlier than the prevailing
mode, with a flattened, obsolete bonnet. Then a supposed
elderly relative came bustling in to inspect the new baby.
She did everything that should not be done; she kissed the
baby effusively; she bounced it violently up and down; she
made faces at it when it cried. Needless to say, the baby in
question was an understudy, a dummy child in fact, which
would not be affected by these misplaced attentions. It was
a good piece of acting and added much to the effectiveness
of the film.

Opposition to the Children's Bureau continued even
after it was firmly established by act of Congress and Presidential signature. Those who had fought against it in vain

now relieved their disappointment by finding fault with all its arrangements and personnel. Julia Lathrop came in for severe criticism. Why, these disgruntled persons asked, was an unmarried woman put at the head of the enterprise, someone who had no children of her own and so could know nothing about them. "A bunch of old maids" they called the staff, ignoring the statistician who was a man and distinguished for his technical skill in a very difficult profession. No word was said publicly about the little girl whom Miss Lathrop had rescued from two disreputable women and whose bringing up and education she had overseen. She did not permit that to be mentioned, and she was only amused by the bitter remarks of certain frustrated citizens.

As a matter of fact the choice of Julia Lathrop as director of this new enterprise could hardly have been bettered. She was an extraordinarily able administrator, as she had shown in the early days. The director was empowered to enlist an advisory committee, and she was fully aware of where she could turn immediately for effective help. Jane Addams was a member of that committee, and Florence Kelley, Lillian Wald and Dr. Devine. These were not all. As time went forward the list was kept filled with the names of eminent leaders in similar work.

The bureau's small appropriation was spent wisely and adroitly, supporting the most necessary steps first, leaving the less pressing matters until later, until an extended plan of attack was made on the dangers that were besetting children everywhere.

Nor did Julia Lathrop and her helpers sit comfortably in their Washington office, waiting for results of their work to be recognized. They went out to meet results and got them. Julia was in great demand as a speaker and justly so. Of all the qualities that she brought to her new responsibilities the greatest was perhaps her glowing personality. She spoke well, convincingly and engagingly. Her evident beauty, the grace and distinction of her person, coupled with the earnestness of her own conviction were irresistible to most of her hearers. Some still sought to heckle her from the audience, but she met them all with a ready and sparkling wit. "Yes, I am that old maid you are all talking about," she would say on beginning a speech. "You are disturbed because I do not have a child. But after all I *was* one for quite a long time."

She traveled tirelessly, to speak at all opportunities. Sometimes it was to explain her work and the need to support it to sophisticated audiences. The Children's Bureau had a unique position: it was the first organization set up by the national government for the welfare of its people, in this instance its small ones. Those who worked with and understood social needs had been saying that a day must come when state and county agencies could not cope with the task and it would take the whole government to do it.

The reason that America was lagging behind other nations in its capacity to take care of its mothers and children lay in America's unmeasured and ignored mass of poverty, more especially in the industrial poor. Now there was an enterprise belonging to the whole country, and the whole country should know of it. Julia Lathrop and the other members of her staff traveled everywhere to see that it did. Much of the time Miss Lathrop and Dr. Meigs went together, she to lecture and explain the nature of her work, her doctor associate to receive mothers and examine babies and give specific advice.

In the country districts, where so little had been done earlier, the travel could be adventurous. Members of the bureau staff would get off the train at a lonely railroad whistle-stop in the Kentucky hills, to be confronted by a rough and ready supporter of their work, mounted and leading a pair of saddled mules as the only means of travel into the back country. Or Children's Bureau representatives would hold meetings in a remote prairie homesteader's cabin or schoolhouse, where the mothers would come flocking, bringing their babies, to sit in rows with worn hands folded in calico laps, listening to the real advice that was so different from the lore of the old midwives who had helped bring their babies into the world. Julia Lathrop knew how to reach them, how to make them feel that here was real interest in their problems. She taught her fellow workers to do the same. Many years ago she said in an interview with a reporter in Washington that someday it would be possible "to declare war on poverty itself."

The Children's Bureau had no legal authority; its mission was to conduct research and distribute information. But such a mandate covered a wide field. Not only the facts of babies' sicknesses and deaths were counted, but the causes of such illnesses and deaths were bound to be examined too. And certainly the work was not to stop with babies, although they seemed to be in the greatest need of attention. It considered the lot of older children too — their education, their chance of development, "their vital efficiency," as Florence Kelley had said before a congressional committee, "their educational opportunity, their future industrial and civic value." In short, everything that made for giving America good citizens was to be the business of the bureau.

Those vested interests which resisted the creation of the Children's Bureau because of suspicions that it would lay hands on child labor were quite right. It did. It looked into and aired the truth about the conditions under which over-young workers were toiling — the little boys in the deep mines sorting slate out of the coal with bleeding hands, the little girls sitting up late hours in suffocating rooms making artificial flowers, the children working under the hot sun setting onions, the children working in factories at danger-ous machines. Although some progress had already been made in the long battle against child labor, it was still far from enough and more long effort was yet to come.

By 1917, efforts of the bureau and others had brought about a national Child Labor Law. The task of administer-ing it and seeing that it was enforced was given to the Children's Bureau, its first legal duty beyond the gathering of information. But the law did not forbid child labor entirely. That was not thought to be practical. At Hull House two sisters were now residents, Grace and Edith Abbott, both showing great ability and great devotion to social betterment. Jane Addams called them "her two good 'abits." Julia Lathrop appointed Grace her assistant with the special task of administering this new law.

Like those good laws which had gone before it, this one was declared unconstitutional after nine months. Grace Abbott stayed on as a member of the bureau staff, however, and succeeded Julia Lathrop in 1921. Certain measures mitigating child labor did follow, but only in limited degree. We can see how blind people in the past have been. In what ways, we wonder, are we being blind now?

A discerning officer in the Post Office Department one day directed a letter to Julia Lathrop which was addressed

"To Uncle Sam." It was from a little girl called Kathryn and requested Uncle Sam to "send a baby brother whenever you have any in." It was one challenge which, unfortunately, the Children's Bureau was not able to meet.

XIV

The Coliseum

As yet not very well known nationally, the young politician
Theodore Roosevelt had been more or less forced to be
McKinley's Vice President. Later he made his distinguished record as the assassinated President's successor.
After being elected for a second term he had, following
George Washington's example, tactfully withdrawn from
seeking a third, although technically he had been elected
only once and had not had the whole of two terms. T.R.
quietly disappeared from before the public eye on the day
of his successor's inauguration, and went off to bury himself
in distant jungles on a big-game hunting expedition. But in
1912, four years later, at the end of that successor's single
term, he returned.

He was a picturesque and glamorous figure still, with his
record of Rough Rider victory in the Spanish-American
War, his vigorous measures concerning the Panama Canal,
his calling of a National White House Conference on
Children's Welfare in 1909. There were now new stories to
tell of his adventures in tropical jungles. Plunging once

more into public life he became highly dissatisfied with the way in which Republican politics were being conducted, especially, he said, the method by which the current Republican nomination for President had been obtained. Since his fellow Republicans did not listen to his criticisms as he felt they should, he made a very bold decision. He would set up a third party and conduct a Presidential campaign on his own.

He was a skilled politician and also a man of many ideas and of bold enterprise in striking out in new directions. His plans for the coming campaign were carefully laid out and contained a wholly new feature. Women did not yet have the vote, but he had friends and admirers among women everywhere and he was well aware of what influence they could exert, even without the ballot. He had a deep, sincere desire to carry forward reforms which he had set going, yet he realized that he did not know enough about procedures in social reform to select the best measures to bring about desired results. No candidate or party had yet framed a maturely considered platform of social reform, even though the need was visible everywhere. Why not invite some of these able women who were carrying on such good service to their fellow men to help him and his campaign committee set up just such a program? And who would be a better helper than Jane Addams? It was true that she had been criticized somewhat in Chicago, but that very fact and her courage in going forward against odds had made her a talked-of and approved figure over the rest of the country.

Jane's political experience had really not been large hitherto, nor had she been very successful in resisting city government corruption and John Power. Even the Illinois

Factory Law had been only a short triumph. But she and those who worked with her were fully convinced that national interest and national law must stand behind reform in the populous cities of industrial America if any real progress was to be made. Much had been accomplished in Europe and in the British colonies. The United States had fallen behind them, weighed down by the indifferent and shortsighted policy of unrestrained capitalists and employers. Jane once defined this policy as "the belief that it is the employer's business to produce goods and that he is not expected to discover and prevent social waste and injury."

Hull House set to work at once to make plans, while Jane and some of her more influential women friends were invited to those mysterious séances of policymakers held behind closed doors, in these cases without the accompaniment of the smoke-laden atmosphere which is supposed to be a required feature of political deliberation. American women did not yet smoke in Jane Addams's day, except for a few who did so in strict privacy, having acquired the habit abroad, and except also for a few old persons who were still addicted to pipes.

What was evolved by the women of Hull House and their consultants was the first all-embracing program for nationally controlled reform. In 1909 Jane Addams had been made president of the National Conference of Charities and Corrections, the most powerful organization yet existing for those interested in improving society. There had been misgivings among the older members of this body over such a radical step as the election of a woman to its highest office.

Under her administration a three-year Committee on Occupational Standards was set up, with Florence Kelley as chairman. It was to complete a program for reforms that would permanently improve the work and living conditions of laboring people in America. This committee was invited to a conference with Theodore Roosevelt at Oyster Bay and its program was incorporated by him almost bodily in his new platform for the Progressive Party. It included proposals for drastic changes to be made in wages, hours, safety and health, housing and conditions of working life, compensation or insurance — all these being considered "components of a proper standard of living." The platform also advocated votes for women as a matter of justice.

At first some ladies held back from taking part in deliberations with political committees. Was not politics a battleground where the truly refined had no place? But led by Jane Addams they quickly saw that here was at last an exceptional opportunity for bettering society, which must not be wasted. Younger and older workers were ready at last to come forward and do their best. The women's clubs of Chicago had developed many able speakers, and a good group of these agreed to do their part.

Jane described the excited tension that filled Chicago when the Progressive Party gathered for its nominating convention in August of 1912. Delegates came from all over the country, many of them from the ranks of those interested in social reform, since now as never before there was a direct invitation to them "to throw their measures into the life of the nation itself," as Jane put it.

With a few of the women leaders of Chicago, Jane lived at the Congress Hotel, where the headquarters of the new party were located. Proceedings were a trifle confused at times since new precedents had to be established, and many of the delegates were young and untried. Jane conscientiously sat in on the platform committee meetings, hesitating a little sometimes over policies other than those of reform, concerning which she was called upon to give her vote. She did not enjoy voting for "the building of two battleships a year, sending an international agreement for the limitation of naval forces, and the setting up of fortifications for the Panama Canal." She did her full part courageously and seriously however, and lent her common sense and the wisdom of experience to the Progressive Party's program for better things. The day came when the committee work was over, the last delegates had arrived and the Progressive Party convention opened. In the end it took only three days to nominate their candidates for President and Vice President, to adopt the official platform and to get through the accompanying conglomeration of formal speeches. The immense Chicago Coliseum had, in 1912, no loudspeakers, so speeches had to be shouted above a continuous bustle of people moving to and fro, talking in ordinary voices, and paying little attention to any but the most distinguished speakers.

Theodore Roosevelt had asked Jane to do one thing more than take part in formulating his platform. Would she make the speech seconding his nomination? Mindful of what he was in a position to do for society, she agreed. She had addressed public meetings before, but never such an enormous throng as this. The huge Coliseum was packed to its highest seats with a mosaic of white faces, fluttering palm-leaf fans, solidly seated humanity. Far above, banners were wavering in the hot drafts. But at last the delegates and the great audience were quiet. No one neglected to listen when Jane Addams spoke.

Theodore Roosevelt, like many another of her contemporaries, had at one time been severely critical of Jane Addams, having differed violently with some of the ideas in her book *Newer Ideals of Peace*. He had soon put that passage between them out of his mind, however, nor did she bear him any grudge because of it. Now she gave Roosevelt his just due and spoke her confidence in his being able to carry out their mutual hopes of reform. Her speech was well received. We cannot doubt that it was refreshingly different from the ordinary political orations of that day. T.R. was launched as a Presidential candidate with the hearty backing of what looked like a great number of supporters.

Jane and her associates more than made good their promises to stand by him through the coming campaign. They went up and down the land on the campaign train, speaking for him in the cities and in the country towns, always making clear that it was his social policy for which they were working, pointing out how deeply needed it was. It was a novel sight to the voters of the land to see women working so vehemently in any public cause. They were effective even if untried, none so much so as Jane. This was one of the occasions when she displayed her rare capacity for doing a large number of varied things exceedingly well.

The campaign was unusual and of high-pressure quality because of two of the personalities involved, for T.R. and Woodrow Wilson were each rather specialized characters. Jane Addams understood Theodore Roosevelt thoroughly, knew his shortcomings quite as well as his abilities. He was volatile, changeable, impulsive, but at heart sound and deeply sincere. Many of his innovations, most of them forgotten now, were so sudden as to be startling. By Presidential order he had decreed during his administration that all government employees should have a half-holiday on Saturdays during July and August. It was a preliminary step in the attack on the hitherto inviolate tradition of a six-day week of ten- or twelve-hour days with total indifference to seasonal vacations. There were many shakings of the head over it. Did not such a step mean the danger of "spoiling the working classes"? There could be no doubt, however, that the President was entirely within his constitutional rights in issuing such an order and comfort was gathered by employers in the thought that government employees were not to be rated exactly as the working class. At least, the innovation had not come about through the demands of trade unions.

Roosevelt's practically single-handed intervention in the Russian-Japanese War, giving two exhausted combatants the opportunity to cease fighting without loss of face, was an achievement dear to Jane's heart. She was already dedicated to peace in its most abstract and far-reaching conception. It is true that his resulting receipt of the Nobel Prize for Peace was a little incongruous for one of such openly belligerent impulse, but it was well deserved. His attempts, the first made by a Presidential administration, against the mushroom growth, through combination, of tremendous corporations with almost unlimited power were also, in Jane's eyes, a valiant step against the industrial evils which she and Hull House had been resisting and publicizing for so long. She was willing indeed to lift her voice for this spokesman who had taken up the program for social betterment. At the height of the campaign Roosevelt was shot, but not very seriously wounded, and the other candidates refrained from any activity until he had recovered.

When Jane spoke in Leadville, Colorado, before a large

group of miners she was able to convince them, to their surprise, that the problems of wages and hours could be political matters, something to be settled by vote, not by violence. She could see even beyond what trade unions could accomplish. She has said that she "happily relished the excitement and the comradeship of a like-minded group," which the campaign afforded in compensation for the discomfort and fatigue of constant travel and incessant speaking. Her assigned field included the two Dakotas, Iowa, Nebraska, Oklahoma, Colorado, Kansas and Missouri, and was conscientiously covered.

People told her after the election that she personally had undoubtedly brought a million votes to Roosevelt. She scoffed at this, saying that the number was greatly exaggerated. Whether it was or not was finally of no significance, for even that addition was not enough. It is a perilous matter in American politics to split a party. Both sections of Republicans went down to defeat and the Democratic candidate, Woodrow Wilson, president of Princeton and governor of New Jersey, came to office. The social program of the Progressive Party was swept away in the general landslide.

A certain adage is sometimes misquoted to the effect that "There is no use running after spilt milk." Jane was probably mindful of it when she said of the cherished reform plan, "The time was not ripe for it." Hull House must once more muster its patience as best it could. No such long step in the direction of social improvement on a national scale would be taken for a considerable time.

The widespread explanations of the Progressive plans for reform had some permanent results. Measures for bettering the lives of deprived people, Jane has said, "were discussed up and down the land as only party politics can be discussed, in the remotest farmhouses to which the rural free delivery brought the weekly newspaper." It was true that a very different atmosphere of opinion concerning social change was spreading throughout the country and the whole society which it contained. The settlements were not the only sources of energy and ideas for improving the lot of their neighbors, although much of the knowledge of what was needed and how the problems were to be met emanated from them. Charitable organizations multiplied and, what was more, organized their plans to administer aid constructively and intelligently instead of haphazardly as had been done earlier. Besides the neighborly settlement visitors, the social worker began to appear, sent by churches and charitable societies, at first as a volunteer, later employed by private organizations, later still by county and state boards, or by commissions of the legislatures.

To achieve real success in their tasks, workers had to be carefully chosen, and they had to be trained. Such training justly should produce a means of livelihood. Settlements did not undertake to offer it; Hull House certainly did not. Their emphasis was upon action and results. Schools for social workers began to be founded: the Chicago School of Civics and Philanthropy, the New York School of Philanthropy, which began as a summer course for social workers set up by the New York Charitable Association. These were followed by an increasing number of others every year. Courses were broadened and the training for social work reached out more and more toward making it a real profession.

It must have cheered Jane Addams to see the numbers of people studying how to serve the needs of others. It

was a task primarily for young people, adaptable, understanding, enterprising and resourceful. An entirely new
profession was opening for them. What she had set on foot
in the beginning was growing with the times into a whole
world of new opportunity for youth, whom she so much
wanted to serve.

Another lasting result of the Progressive campaign was to
alter the public attitude toward Jane Addams. She had
come before the public an able, sincere and eloquent
speaker acclaimed everywhere outside of Chicago. In the
city the hostility to her fell away and people in general,
even the newspapers, saw her again as she really was. If she
could appear in alliance with an ex-President she could
hardly be rated any longer as "a dangerous radical."

When the next Presidential election approached, both
sides asked for her assistance. Charles Evans Hughes, the
Republican candidate, wanted her to make speeches for
him; Woodrow Wilson, running for a second term, asked
for her help also. She firmly declined both invitations, true
to her statement that she spoke only to support carefully
defined and greatly needed reforms. But she was so hard
pressed by both sides to take part in the campaign that she
finally issued a public statement.

After a lifetime of Republican loyalty, she was now
giving her adherence to Woodrow Wilson, since during his
first term he had advocated and put into practice a good
number of the measures she considered necessary. She cited
them in a public letter as "a record of pledges fulfilled."
They were resolutions in support of the rights of labor,
particularly of freedom of contract for seamen, enabling
them to leave their employment if it became intolerable,
which under a tyrannical captain it often could be. Further,

a law had been passed forbidding the products of child labor to be handled by interstate commerce, a small step in the right direction. Another measure provided workmen's compensation to two hundred thousand federal employees. The general principle of the eight-hour day was recognized.

Jane received the following letter from President Wilson: "My dear Miss Addams: I cannot deny myself the pleasure of telling you how proud I am, and how much strengthened I feel that I should have your approval and support."

Jane had constantly maintained that people who came as residents to Hull House did not come to learn to be social workers. Settlements were founded for something else. They were to give immediate and personal help where it was needed, and to develop plans and stimulate action in the cause of social justice. A settlement was not a formalized institution; its purpose was to learn by direct contact with friends and neighbors the ills under which society was suffering and to arouse interest in finding the necessary remedies. Jane was always certain that they could be found.

XV

The Devil Baby

An accident which brought general public notice to Hull House was one that nobody but Jane Addams could have understood or interpreted. She alone had the requisite insight, the affectionate perception and the sense of humor for seeing the real truth. But even she might not have caught the true significance of the strange affair had it not been for her long observation and concern for a certain aspect of the problems of the young.

She and Mary Rozet Smith had made a brief journey abroad to the Middle East after the Progressive campaign. She always returned happily to Hull House — it was home, it was her life. Soon after their return, in the midst of ordinary routine, came a day when three Italian women appeared at the door saying that they wanted to see the Devil Baby which Hull House was sheltering. When they were told that no such baby was there, they insisted that they knew better, they could give full details of his pointed ears, his cloven hoofs, his miniature tail.

He could speak, so the tale ran, from the moment of his

birth, and was shockingly impertinent and profane when he did so. Accounts of his origin varied bewilderingly. One was that a well-brought-up and religious Italian girl was married to an atheist who, seeing a holy picture on the wall, tore it down with imprecations saying that he would rather have the devil in his house than such a thing hanging there. The Devil, overhearing him, took him at his word. A Jewish version went that a man who had six daughters had said he would rather have a devil in his family than another girl, and the Devil promptly granted him his wish. But both versions agreed that the father, like so many other people in trouble, carried the baby straight to Hull House, asking for advice. The people of Hull House, it was reported, promptly prepared to have the child baptized, but when they brought him, wrapped in a shawl, before the priest, they found the shawl empty and were just in time to catch the baby skipping across the backs of the pews, fleeing from the touch of holy water.

The tidings of this amazing arrival spread among the neighbors as rapidly as all news relating to Hull House. As the circles of misinformation extended, people came in dozens, in scores, then in hundreds. For six weeks Hull House was besieged daily and late into the night by trusting souls believing firmly in the Devil Baby and clamoring to see him. Persons of all ages and of all walks of life came to the door, nor could mere curiosity be called their only incentive. Jane Addams talked to them all, pondered the curious incident and finally came to some unexpected conclusions. The presence of so many old women among the sensation seekers seemed to her significant, but of what? She was certain that in those older persons who came, no matter what outward reasons were given for their being there, was a hidden remnant of some superstition, some grotesque loyalty to a legend which they had never overcome.

There was one old woman, a not very distant neighbor, who was completely bedridden and had no one to take her to verify this extraordinary occurrence with her own eyes. Visitors brought her the information that Hull House was denying there was a Devil Baby, was trying to pretend that he did not exist. Unless "Herself" came and told her so, she declared, she would never believe that he was not there. Jane Addams went. She felt so sorry for the poor invalid that she could not help meditating on whether she should humor her by pretending that there was such an inmate at Hull House.

It would have meant so much to the lonely old woman to have a new and startling being to think about, a new tale to tell. But the pathetic old soul, watching so excitedly from her bed as Jane Addams came in, read instantly upon her face the fact that the story was not true. The light died out of her eager eyes; she made no protest against the tidings that the simple presence of "Herself" had brought.

This old person had once owned a prosperous secondhand store, but she had a shiftless drunken husband and a collection of jolly, irresponsible sons. They were all gone now and the store with them, "owing to the drink," as she said resignedly. Her very young grandson alone was left to give her what care and support he could. It hardly seemed that life could deal her another blow, but now it had.

The story that finally became generally accepted was that the father had committed a desperate crime but had never been found out. He married a young wife without telling her about his hidden guilt and when they had their first baby, the personification of his sin confronted him in the form of his diabolical son. The theory that sin would be punished by divine intervention, often preached by the old to the young, was thus being vindicated and the old women were taking comfort in the support given their ideas.

This was why so many of these very old immigrant women continued to be among the most determined seekers after the Devil Baby, and the most difficult to convince that he was not there. Their inevitable presence among the crowds of young people gave Jane Addams her real insight into this strange affair. Over and over again she had seen a family of newcomers arrive in America to seek a better life, bringing along the old grandmother or ancient aunt who could not be left behind, but who could never learn, at such an age, to be an American. The children and grandchildren quickly acquired the new language, became accustomed to the new ways, went to school or got work and set up a new life. A hopeless barrier would grow between them and the old unreconstructed parents or grandparents, a rift which Jane had often tried vainly to explain to both sides in an attempt to bring them together again.

The aged women's tales of the Old Country, tinged with the magic and marvels of cherished superstition, usually met with frank indifference and disbelief in the younger generation. Here at last many old women had thought to find proof that their supernatural stories were to be believed after all, that their recollected store of ancient lore was of value in the end. They would have their moment of triumph if they could only show the Devil Baby to these unbelieving ones.

For weeks the staff of Hull House was occupied all day long in saying "No, there is no use in getting up an excursion from Milwaukee to see him, he isn't here," or "We cannot make reduced rates for showing him, even though you heard of someone who saw him for fifty cents." Unconvinced applicants would reply, "Why do you let so many people believe in it when it isn't there?" or "This is a pretty big place, you could hide it easy enough," or "Why are you still saying it isn't here; are you going to raise the price of admission?"

After four or five weeks the story got into the papers and reporters arrived, not to verify the presence of this strange visitor, but to watch the people who came to inquire. The many unthinking persons who had been so willing to pronounce Hull House "a nest of anarchists" must have felt a little sheepish seeing how easy it was, for slightly simpler minds, to believe that it was the chosen abode of the Devil himself. The story finally died a natural death, but it had shed some illumination on various hidden truths. Jane Addams comforted the disappointed old women as best she could, and tried to make it clear to their young people how natural and pathetic was this frenzy of belief which had taken hold of so many of their elders. It did more than any argument to make the young understand their elders better.

It was Jane's desire "to reveal the humbler immigrant parents to their own children" that led unexpectedly to one of Hull House's most successful enterprises. Walking down the street one sunny spring morning, she saw an old woman sitting on the steps of a tenement house using a distaff, a stick spindle that is one of the most ancient forms of spinning thread or wool. The old woman saw Jane's interest, smiled and held up her spindle. She said that when she had spun enough thread she was going to knit a pair of stockings for her goddaughter. This homely picture of sunshine, industry and content put the beginning of an idea into Jane's creative mind, an idea which presently developed into what came to be called the Hull House Labor Museum.

These older women had brought with them from the Old Country many arts and handicrafts of which America knew very little. There were in the neighborhood of Hull House various sorts of spinning and weaving apparatuses, some very primitive, some beginning to be modernized. These were collected, placed in historic sequence to show progress, and women who had not lost their early skill would presently come to work in a room that Jane provided for them. Here was built up in time a prosperous craft shop that offered handmade articles of all sorts and of exceptionally good workmanship.

Julius Rosenwald, millionaire head of the Sears, Roebuck Company and one of the Hull House trustees, was so struck by the interest and success of this small exhibit of handicrafts in action that he developed the idea 'into a far larger one, an industrial museum which was to show all the products of men's hands aided by industrial machinery. He housed it in the huge old Fine Arts Building, remaining from the World's Fair, which had been left to drop to pieces in spite of its faultless architecture and beautiful proportions. It was one of the most beautiful structures America had so far produced. Rebuilt in stone, it now stands a magnificent monument to American industry, to the creative idea of Julius Rosenwald, incidentally to Hull House and to a little old woman spinning on a tenement step in the spring sun.

Many of the ideas which Jane developed in her analysis

of the beliefs and practices of the older women in immigrant families were embodied in her book *The Long Road of Woman's Memory*. One might think from the title that it is a chapter of autobiography, but it is not. It is a profound discussion of the qualities of memory characteristic of the aged. Next to one other, it was the book in which she took most satisfaction.

The Hull House workshop offered instances again and again of how differences between old and young could be bridged. For instance, an Italian girl named Angelina came every Saturday to a cooking class at Hull House. Her mother came with her, for also on Saturday evenings exhibitions were held in the Labor Museum room, but her daughter always left her at the door. One evening Angelina caught a glimpse of her mother in the midst of a group of chattering friends in the Museum, all consulting her and showing work for her comment. The daughter had been ashamed of her mother's head-handkerchief, her short petticoats and thick boots, and had not liked to be seen with her. But when she saw her mother admired and looked up to as an authority she felt sudden respect. Jane Addams, who saw everything, noted the girl's change of heart. Here was one of the small successes, the minor miracles of Hull House which sustained its founder.

XVI

War and Famine

At the close of the 1916 elections, Woodrow Wilson came into his second term as President, riding on the slogan "He kept us out of war." They were not words of his choosing; the claim was not his own. It was that of his campaign managers. It turned out to be wishful thinking on everyone's part. Conditions abroad and the imperialistic attitude of Germany made it plain that such a mandate could not be fulfilled. In April 1917 the President came before Congress and asked for a declaration of war. The declaration followed at once. By that time scarcely anyone believed that it could be avoided.

War changes everything. All of industry had to be reorganized for maximum production of munitions; unemployment disappeared. The power of labor unions had to be recognized, for the supply of manpower was suddenly far less than the demand, and the union members could have a voice in making their own terms. Prices rose; sugar disappeared almost entirely from the market, not because it was lacking in supply but because every housewife was laying in a store against the chance that it would be. Laws had to be passed with penalties for hoarding it. Every sort of dislocation of normal living followed one upon another.

It is not the purpose of this account to follow in detail Jane Addams's second career, although she did have two. The founding of Hull House and the successful administration of it for forty years, anyone would think was enough for one woman to do. But the striking results of this venture and her ability for leadership had made her a well-known figure, not only all over the United States but also in all English-speaking countries. The disapproval of certain circles in Chicago counted for little against the general admiration for all that she had done. Her second career was that of a leader among women for peace by negotiation and continuous mediation, without resort to arms in international disputes. It embodied the idea that peace could be brought about by concerted action of women all over the world.

As early as 1907 in her book *Newer Ideals of Peace*, Miss Addams voiced her belief that war could and should be outlawed, and in the end done away with entirely. Now, as in all of her active life, she was praised and abused in turn, but she steadily followed the course which she had decided was right. She called herself a pacifist, but she was not one in our recently accepted meaning of the word. She took no part in resistance to her country's war effort once hostilities had irrevocably begun. As the First World War cast its long shadow across Europe, women all over the world began to organize, to hold meetings and congresses to debate on how to eliminate war fom human society. It was natural that Jane Addams, the best-known leader of women's movements, should be chosen almost automatically to be the parliamentary head of this one.

She had been the first woman president of the largest and most important association among social reformers, the National Conference of Charities and Corrections. Various conservative members of that body complained against such an innovation, but the brilliance of her inaugural address had silenced them. She had addressed the gathered thousands at the Progressive convention, a moment for which no previous experience had really prepared her. Now again she was meeting a situation quite new to her, facing and ordering the business for the thousands of women representatives at the Women's Congress. They gathered from all over the world, from nations on both sides of the surging hostilities, varying in ideas, in sentiments, in language. Under her presiding hand speeches were made, arguments completed, motions carried in steady and controlled action. All this was done by women not used to parliamentary procedure, presided over by a woman almost as unused to it as the rest.

It would be impossible to tell in any short compass how much her cool and wise administration really accomplished. It is enough to report that some of the ideas which developed under debate in the Women's Congress at the Hague, formulated by a committee of that same congress, were submitted as resolutions to President Wilson and ultimately appeared as part of his famous Fourteen Points. On the basis of that document the belligerents of the First World War were later persuaded to open negotiations for peace.

In the interval when war was so visibly approaching,

JANE ADDAMS

when hostilities in Europe were getting under way, a generation that had not known military conflict clutched at straws of hope that war would pass the United States by. It was then that Jane Addams and her fellow workers for peace were praised. But when the truth became clear that no negotiation was possible with political dictators moved purely by the lust for conquest, when war had descended upon a nation that did not want it, when "he kept us out of war" was a true slogan no longer, then criticism and abuse arose clamorously once more and Jane was vilified as she had been so many times before.

She did not raise her voice to defend herself, even though she spoke eloquently in many places in America and Europe to defend the ideal of peace. It is evident from those speeches that her belief in the cause rested largely in her interest and concern for youth. The terrible waste of young men that war involved laid in the dust her hopes of making a better world for them.

She was away from Hull House for long periods at a time, but her heart and mind were with her work there just the same. Her fellow workers were helping needy families whose wage-earners were at the front, and comforting households where a gold star in the window showed that one member would never come back. Young men of the neighborhood who enlisted had their last meal at Hull House, and said their goodbyes in its familiar court where they had played as boys.

The Women's Peace Party, which was later organized as the Women's International League for Peace and Freedom, planned to hold a meeting in Paris at the same time that the Peace Conference of the victorious allies discussed the terms to be presented to the defeated Germans. This

was not found to be possible so the simultaneous meeting
was held in Switzerland at Zurich. When the terms of the
peace treaty were finally announced, the Women's League
presented the first comment upon them uttered by any
public body. "The International Congress of Women ex-
presses its deep regret that the terms of peace proposed at
Versailles should so seriously violate the principles upon
which alone a just and lasting peace can be secured."

Miss Addams was one of a delegation of five chosen at
Zurich to present the league's resolutions to the Peace
Conference in Paris. While she was there she consulted
with Herbert Hoover, who was at that time head of the
relief organization which was feeding the starving people of
Germany and Belgium. She had some talk with him which
was to bear fruit later, and dined at his house. Later she
said of Hoover that his office in Paris was "the one reasonable spot in the midst of widespread confusion."

Contention and disagreement were everywhere. The
Fourteen Points had voiced statesmanship and generosity,
but generosity disappeared in the struggle to take advantage of a much-dreaded enemy. Woodrow Wilson, in spite
of heroic effort, was not able to achieve his high-minded
purposes. He got his Covenant of the League of Nations,
he saw the German people rid themselves of the Hohenzol-
lerns, he got the return of Alsace-Lorraine to France, but he
got little else, not even the consent of his own country to
take part in the new league.

But the Hoover Commission was doing memorable
work. Famine grimly treads on the heels of war. When the
smoke had cleared away and communications were reestab-
lished, it was discovered that nearly all of Europe was
hungry and a large proportion was starving. Conditions in

France were hard, in Belgium worse, in Germany worst of all.

Five days after peace had been officially declared, Jane Addams, Mary Rozet Smith and Alice Hamilton were sent by the American Friends Service Committee to inspect conditions in Germany and report on the needs there. Here was a more familiar Jane Addams, as the three friends visited schools, hospitals, and cottages. She had a smile for all as the children stood in orderly rows before her, "just a line of moving skeletons," she says, "their legs like pipe-stems, their shoulder blades like wings." The old people were worse off still, for they had felt they must not eat when they could contribute nothing in return.

The English Quakers, as members of the Friends Service Committee, had brought with them thirty thousand dollars collected as "gifts of love," and had purchased through the Hoover Commission thirty-five tons of condensed milk, seventeen tons of sugar and other foodstuffs in proportion, which were available for distribution in Germany. It was a mere drop in the bucket of the desperate want, but it made the journey less heartrending to have something to offer.

Herbert Hoover, at the head of the Relief Commission and a Quaker himself, achieved magnificent success in the almost hopeless task of saving a whole generation from the lasting effects of those years of starvation. The three women from Hull House went home knowing just what work was before them. Sent out on their return by Hoover's Washington office they traveled widely and spoke every-where, urging the collection of money for relief and the production and conservation of food to the last possible ounce. Rationing had been established in America, and uncomfortable and inconvenient it was, causing much superficial complaint. But it was a trivial hardship compared with what people abroad were suffering. It was up to Jane and her helpers to make people see that the responsibility of a war does not end with victory. To plead for money and food for the people of Germany was a highly unpopular task, perhaps the most unpopular of all Jane's undertakings. But she met with success in spite of that. Her honesty of purpose, her gift of moving speech, in the end prevailed even though she was refused a hearing in many places where the name of Jane Addams would once have opened every door.

Hull House itself, as she found on her return, continued to meet its war responsibilities, and those that came after, with determination and valor. The office of the local draft board was at Hull House. The neighborhood problems were great where so many of the households had lost their main supporters. The long absence of a father of a family often made for lack of discipline at home, especially when the mother went out to work to add to the shrunken income.

The government had established a fair and just system of soldiers' insurance, formulated by Judge Mack of Chicago, who had done so much in establishing the first juvenile court. But the collection of benefits was an elaborate and intricate process, as government procedure tends to be, and was often beyond the understanding of those to whom English was not yet a fully familiar tongue.

Three weeks before the war ended, Jane's oldest nephew, son of her sister Mary, was killed by a shell in northern France. She had always been very close to his mother; she was equally close to her nephew, who was only twelve years younger than herself. After the war, when she was on her way to a conference in Zurich, she was asked by the Red Cross to go on a tour of inspection of the devastated regions in the northern sector of France. She paused on her way to look for his grave and finally found it, the third in the row of one of those endless lines of white crosses that write their tragic message across the green French countryside.

Hull House had been discovering that war produces great numbers of deeply disturbed young people, who must find counsel and reassurance somewhere. For many of them there was the experience of love stimulated to rapid climax by the knowledge of what lay beyond, of sudden and often little-considered marriage and immediate parting, which could well be forever. One solace was that there was now work for everyone. Unemployment vanished as thousands — mounting up in the end to millions — of the able-bodied workers were called abroad.

Hull House had been built with a dormer window on the second floor over the doorway. This gave space to the Octagon Room within, which was Jane Addams's office. There she was always available to anyone who wished to see her. Countless numbers came there to speak of what was in their deepest hearts — the sorrowing, the bewildered, the bitter, the rebellious, those struggling with any of the million problems which life can offer. All these troubled ones partook of the ready understanding, the tireless sympathy, and the unfailing wisdom of that universal friend. More needed her now than ever before.

War, actual war, comes on overnight and alters everything. Peace even more suddenly can do the same thing. But peace, when it arrived, brought a multiplication of problems of its own. Along with all the rejoicing there were

"That universal friend"
in her sixties

various difficult readjustments to be made. In some of the overhasty marriages the young husband and wife could not begin where they left off, since they had scarcely begun before. Children who had never seen their fathers or had only the haziest recollection of them, when confronted by returning strangers, often resented them.

Then there were the war brides from abroad. They were not allowed to come over to America at once, since space on shipboard was used to bring all the soldiers back as soon as possible. When it was finally arranged that the women — French, Belgian and German — could come, social workers met them at the dock and took them to their new homes. A woman, young then, tells of being one of these volunteers and of taking into her car one of the passengers, a girl of dignity, poise and evident culture. The address she gave as her destination was rather surprising, since it was in a poorer part of the city. When they reached the place the newcomer got out, looked about her in some astonishment, then climbed the stairs of the tenement which bore the number of her address. The girl who had brought her waited for a little, full of vague misgivings and unwilling to leave the situation as it stood. In a very short time the French girl came down again. "Take me back to the ship," she said. "I am going home."

This same thing could have happened a number of times. A young man in uniform, held to the neatness, orderliness and sobriety of military discipline, can be quite different back in his own environment.

There was a brief, shocking upsurge in crime, especially of youthful crime. War is a brutal business and brutality can be contagious and lasting. The excitement of war held over into the days of peace, into the return of young men to their old routine jobs, into the company of people who knew so little of what war was really like and what these boys had been through. Jane Addams had always understood that what looked like wantonness of spirit was really a part of being young. It was now at its highest pitch. Robberies were frequent, battles with the police occurred again and again. Discontent with the results of the war and a feeling that all the effort had been useless contributed to the lawlessness.

The advent of peace also brought its shock to industry. Manufacturing had been highly stepped up, even before the war, to supply France and Great Britain with munitions. It had expended supreme efforts when the United States took part in hostilities. Now it came to a sudden halt. Thousands of young men were coming home looking for the jobs they had once filled. They were hardly prepared to find them occupied by women.

XVII

The Goose Hangs High

Although at the end of World War I women occupied more places in industry than anyone had ever thought they could fill, many were glad to give up their jobs and go back to domestic life. But there was, nonetheless, unemployment everywhere. The winter of 1918–1919 was a very hard one, and further, it brought the influenza epidemic which extended across the land.

The sickness began before the end of the war, coming over from Europe, seeming to grow more deadly as it spread. The crowded army camps were hotbeds for the development of fresh infections; troopships carrying their overload of soldiers abroad were often a shambles of the sick and dying when they docked at a French port. But it was so necessary to pour reinforcements into the armies abroad at this late, critical moment of the war, that it appeared to be the wiser policy to hurry the men overseas no matter what was the death rate on board. It would save lives in the end — and it did. War is a ruthless business.

The influenza struck the vigorous young people, more

than the old or the very young; it was particularly fatal to young mothers. It was swift in its deadly work; the person who sat next to you at the Red Cross work table one day was absent the next and two days later would be gone. Impromptu hospitals were set up in public and club buildings, sometimes even in rows of tents, to take in all the stricken patients. By the heroic efforts of exhausted doctors and worn-out nurses, many were saved.

The sickness spread like prairie fire over the whole country. Cities were full of it, small towns riddled with it, lonely ranch houses in the Far West were often so stricken that neighbors, breaking in when they saw no smoke in the chimneys, would find a whole family dead, with perhaps only the baby living, and it near to starvation. Among the crowded, unsanitary tenements of Chicago's West Side, Hull House workers were overwhelmed with duties to the sick, the dying, the dead and the bereft. Were not all of these *neighbors*, and was not this a part of the work for which Hull House had been founded?

Added to the pressure of work and the distress all about her, was Jane Addams's revived unpopularity for having been a self-admitted pacifist, also for advocating material help to stricken Germany, and for her tendency to support unpopular causes in general. That she so often proved in the end to be right in such support was to many of her detractors, and especially to the newspapers, most irritating of all. She always suffered deeply under public disapproval; she was a person with no self-righteousness and little self-assurance to sustain her.

An important Englishwoman, Maude Royden, coming to the United States to lecture, said of her, "In 1912 I learned that it was unsafe to mention Jane Addams's name in a public speech unless you were prepared for an interruption, because a mere reference to her provoked such a storm of applause. . . . After the War, I realized with a shock how complete was the eclipse of her fame — her popularity had swiftly and completely vanished. How well I remember when I spoke in America in 1922 and 1923, what silence greeted the name of Jane Addams. The few faithful who tried to applaud only made the silence more depressing." Jane's only defense was her valiant heart.

What distressed Miss Addams almost more than anything else was the obstinate persistence of interracial intolerance which was an aftermath of the war. Hatred is an unhealthy passion which the war had deliberately nourished to a high degree. A picture in *Punch* during the war, passing for a joke — a very grim one — was a "study of a German family having its daily morning hate." Hatred of enemies moved now to hatred and suspicion of all foreigners. Jane had become very earnest in her belief that international friendship was a possible thing, since she had seen immigrants from so many different countries coming in harmony to enjoy themselves at Hull House. Now she must watch rifts and feuds and dark mistrust arise between those who could so well have been friends.

Many of the early immigrant families had prospered and moved to better parts of Chicago. The empty tenement homes were being filled by Mexicans and Negroes. Race riots arose at the end of the war, mainly on account of unemployment. Hull House had always stood without question for complete equality among all comers. This bristling intolerance was something that hurt Jane deeply.

Finally those distressing and confused years immediately following the war passed. Business took an upturn and began to hum again. Hull House was prospering as the country was, as Chicago was. Throughout, some stalwarts had stood steadily by Jane Addams; they were joined now by a few others with renewed faith in her. No new Hull House buildings had been put up during the war, but the whole block was now covered, and at the moment there was no special need for others. The income and expenditure of the settlement was $60,000 at the beginning of the war; by 1922 it was $70,000; and in 1929, when it was forty years old, it received $95,000. It could have used far more.

Jane's personal income, derived from her father's estate and from her being what Leo Tolstoy had designated "an absentee landlord," was now less than one hundred dollars a month. But she received payments for books and articles and for lecturing, and so could pay for her own living at Hull House and give away any margin to the different needs which were so thick around her. She had returned from abroad to see the country enter on the wild joyride of the twenties, when business prosperity soared and almost everybody who had any spare money speculated in the stock market. A good number who did not have any spare funds did the same. New industries were blossoming and prices were steadily rising. Vast numbers of people, contemplating their paper profits, thought of themselves as brilliant financiers and told themselves that they would surely sell out after making a reasonable fortune. Very few did; the temptation to go a little farther was always too great.

An old-time expression, "The goose hangs high," is used to denote large and comfortable prosperity. It implies cheerful holiday company, a blazing fire in a deep old-fashioned fireplace with the fat goose hanging from the

hook above, roasting for the impending feast. It was pecu-
liarly appropriate to this time of artless finance. The whole
economy was riding headlong toward a fearful fall, but
nobody admitted it.

The question of child labor once more came to the fore.
There had not been much agitation against it during the
war. With so many workers at the front, with the pressure
for utmost production, it seemed to be no time to continue
the attack. When the men from overseas returned, all
seeking jobs, great numbers of the children were discharged
and it appeared as though the problem might at last take
care of itself. Yet the needs of the war had so greatly
stimulated industry and shown how much production was
possible that it never went back permanently to its former
levels. With so much money being made and spent in
recklessly extensive buying, production had to expand with
it. As a result child labor almost automatically intensified
again. Once more it was necessary to battle against it, for
now with such profits rolling in it seemed to be more firmly
established than ever.

The Children's Bureau took up the campaign as an
essential duty. It was now extending its research and issuing
report after report about boys eleven to fifteen years old
working in mines in air thick with coal dust. Other children
were toiling in home industries, stringing beads, putting
snaps on cards, paid five to ten cents an hour, working nine
hours a day, sometimes as much as fourteen in the rush
season. Various states passed laws to restrain and regulate
such unfair employment, but when these were enforced
they put those states at a disadvantage, since industries
elsewhere could undersell those who observed the law.
There were conferences over strategy, discussions every-

where, committees established, hearings before Congress. Jane and her associates spoke, wrote and testified again and again.

Through the constant debate there began to emerge the fact that state control of child labor could never give full regulation, and that to avoid competition there must be a uniform law for all. The success of the Children's Bureau under Julia Lathrop seemed to indicate that here also was a problem which only the central authority could handle. A bill was presented in Congress for an amendment to the Constitution, to put an end to child labor once and for all.

The same arguments against such a measure were produced, just as before. The manufacturers, defending their vested interests, fearing the threat of a rise in cost of production, fought to their utmost to defeat the amendment. The propaganda this time was more subtle, and more effective. It was built on the grounds of states' rights. The central government should not be given such power to interfere with the industry of the several states; it would be the entering wedge of more and more authority in the hands of Congress and the President.

A children's strike in a factory in Allentown, Pennsylvania, and the publicizing of the conditions of hardship and exploitation under which they were working, gave sudden force to the campaign and the bill for the addition to the Constitution passed in 1924. It remained now for two-thirds of the forty-eight states to ratify it.

Those who had so long dedicated their efforts to social reform fought for this ratification as they had never fought before. Women's suffrage had been achieved in 1920, an acknowledgment of how important women had been to

industry and to society when the men were involved elsewhere. But even with the force of the vote finally in their
hands, the women could not tip the balance of the scale for
the Child Labor Amendment. Enormous fortunes and ever
greater concentration of capital were on the other side,
against ratification. Skilled lobbyists, experienced purveyors
of propaganda, asserted that now, with prosperity returning
at last, it would risk disaster to withdraw so large a part of
the working force of established industry. The fact was that
so much money was being made that people were eager to
make even more and were deaf and blind to the real truths
of the situation, truths which Jane Addams and a cohort of
other speakers were trying vainly to put before the public.
No one would stop to see that a generation which had lost
125,000 of its best young men could ill afford to stand by
and watch the wastage of its young children.

The wages paid to these small workers were often less
than a dollar a day, and their occupation was costing them
their health and their schooling. There were regulations
about their going to school, but these were easy to avoid.
At one factory in the South the manager professed himself
so open to inspection, so ready to welcome all who came to
examine the working of his establishment, that he raised
the flag as a sign of welcome whenever an inspector arrived
or was reported to be on the way. It was a secret signal for
all the working children to slip out and go home. It was not
likely that a stranger would notice the still spinning, un-
attended machines, or the half-wound bobbins dropped
upon the floor.

It had been possible to get the measure for the amendment through Congress, but the more detailed and personal campaigns in the states for ratifying it were another

matter indeed. By 1928 the question of ratification had been up before all the forty-eight states. Twenty-five had ratified, one state beyond half, but a Constitutional amendment called for a two-thirds affirmative vote. The Child Labor Amendment was lost, wrecked on that same fact which Jane Addams had first learned in the campaign against Alderman John Power. It was of no use to pass a law for reform when the people were not ready for it.

Another such amendment, promising great things, illus- trated the same truth, and though it had a longer life, came to its end for the same reason. This was the amendment establishing Prohibition. It had been born of a great wave of enthusiasm which swept Prohibition into law in 1920. It turned out to be a measure which people in large part found that after all they did not really believe in and were unwilling to obey. Jane and others like her could see the great benefits of Prohibition to the laboring man, and to his wife and children, to the poor at large, to those who had slipped into the habit of drunkenness because it was the only available relaxation and recreation in a life over- crowded by stultifying labor. Lillian Wald and her associ- ates at the Henry Street Settlement in New York stood firmly by it also. Only those closely associated with the poor could see Prohibition's intention, but it was not possible even for them to foresee, and even less to prevent, the desperate consequences it was to bring about. The disastrous results arose not from the measure itself, but from the total disregard of it.

The law was broken everywhere at all levels of society, while more and more money was made by the purveyors of illegal liquor. A whole underworld took possession of the business of importing, manufacturing and supplying it.

This underworld was dominated by ignorant but nonetheless shrewd and totally unscrupulous leaders, each with his own gang and all presently at war with one another for the domination of the illicit trade. In the drastic history of the next few years the experience, even the memory, of Prohibition was to be swept away. It was one of the favorite criticisms of the Child Labor Amendment, brought up whenever there was discussion of reviving it again, that it would fare no better than had Prohibition. But even such talk also gradually died.

Jane Addams had been spared some of the excitements experienced by Chicagoans during those tumultuous days of the early nineteen-twenties. She had been persuaded by her doctors and her friends to take a long vacation. People who saw her then, when asked for some recollected detail about her, almost invariably say first, "She looked tired." She nearly always looked tired; her pictures show it. She was tired, since every day she spent herself to the limit of her strength.

She had been called to the Netherlands in 1923 to preside over a meeting of the Congress of Women at the Hague. It was evident to all that Miss Addams was worn out by the pressure of her activities and that she should find some real relaxation and rest. So after the meeting she and Mary Rozet Smith decided to turn their faces eastward across Europe and travel around the world. Foreign travel had always pleased her and seemed to afford her rest. "I don't think I am adventurous," she said, although not very truly, "but I have always liked to get about."

She was hailed everywhere she went as a famous figure and a loved person. She was asked to speak on countless occasions about "Women and Peace." Newspapers carried

long articles on her work and in praise of her accomplishments; she was acknowledged as the world leader of
women's participation in public affairs. She declared cheerily, without a trace of bitterness, "To some it almost seems
as if an internationally minded person should be defined as
a friend in every country except his own."

She visited India, where suffrage had just been given to
women and where she wished greatly to see a veiled Indian
woman casting a vote and was surprised to observe how
easily and naturally she did it. She had an accident in
China, and was taken seriously ill in Japan, where she had
to be operated on. The Imperial Court sent messages to the
hospital to inquire how she was. It had been intended that
a reception would be held in her honor by the Emperor and
Empress, but this had to be given up. In three weeks Jane
was able to travel and to set out for home. She was always
glad to be turning homeward, perhaps because unexpected
things might be going on there.

Matters were moving smoothly, however, when the
travelers returned to Hull House. The tide of prosperity
was still high. Jane's friends could afford to be generous, so
that there was no need for those efforts at money-getting of
which she said so little and thought so much. There were
always new opportunities in all directions; there were always people waiting to see Miss Addams and get her
advice. The organization had now received the gift of
seventy-two acres of ground with ten buildings at Wauke-
gan, all given by Mrs. Bowen. The place was to be organized as the Bowen Country Club where residents and
members could go for relaxation and rest. For many of the
children who went there to spend a week of outdoor play

breathing country air, it was the first glimpse of any world outside a city slum.

Hull House affairs were still so well in hand that early in the next year Jane took a trip to Mexico with Lillian Wald. Mary Rozet Smith joined them in Mexico City and the three, who were the best sort of sightseers, greatly enjoyed the picturesque mud-thatched huts, the men "looking like brigands," the winding roads up the mountainsides and the activity and color everywhere. They had an interview with President Calles, during which Lillian Wald reproached him for his policy against the Church.

As this astonishing decade in American history moved beyond the mid-twenties, various clouds began to sweep up from the horizon to darken the atmosphere of the still high-riding prosperity. Professional social workers, of whom there were now many all over the country, began to report scattered pockets of unemployment for which there seemed to be no logical explanation. This threatening element in the midst of what still seemed to be a safe and lively economic era was to grow and spread, leading to staggering events. Not even the wisest students of social and economic theory were prepared for the extent of the coming catastrophic changes. But just before the gathering storm broke, an episode occurred in Jane Addams's personal life that changed the whole aspect of her position before the Chicago public.

XVIII

The Furniture Mart

Those clouds which had been slowly gathering over a society happily absorbed in its delusion of riches were beginning to puzzle a few people, particularly those interested in the poor. A group of Jane Addams's friends got together and suggested a consultation to discuss a question too serious to be ignored. Would Miss Jane Addams consent to be the center of such a meeting? She would, she said, but urged that the discussion "remain theoretical and philosophic." It was her way of saying that she hoped the occasion would not be made a personal one.

Not long before there had been a sudden and vicious attack upon her by a national society which should have known better. It had gone so far beyond the bounds of reasonable justice that an upsurge of protest rose even among those who had lent themselves easily to little-considered criticism of her. The question began to be asked in more and more places: If these accusations were so palpably false, had not many of the earlier ones been the same? Had all this former abuse of her really been justified?

During the war Jane Addams had stood firmly for mediation and negotiated peace. In the light of sober reflection now that the war was over, was that in itself so evil a thing? She and her following had never really interfered with the great military effort against an enemy that was threatening the welfare of all mankind. It might be time to think again. It might, indeed, be time to see her as a woman who had devoted her whole life to doing good, who had faced and endured abuse without rancor or complaint, who had not allowed controversy to be stirred up by combating the untrue accusations hurled against her.

A prominent newspaper owner, whose policy had long been one of continual attack upon Jane Addams, came to see the truth suddenly when he was on his deathbed. He sent word to her that he now knew she had been right-minded in all she did, and expressed his sorrow for being so wrong. Public opinion in her favor grew like a rolling snowball. Regret for former criticism of her grew ever faster. Chicago was ready to make common apology to Jane Addams.

The dinner meeting planned for discussion of current social conditions, set for January 1927, lost all semblance of its avowed purpose and turned into a huge testimonial for one person. Social progress was mentioned only incidentally, the real subject of all the speechmaking was Miss Jane Addams.

Fifteen hundred persons had places at the dinner, with further hundreds turned away because they had not made reservations in time. The Furniture Mart, the building which had the largest floor space in the city, would hold no more. Letters and telegrams arrived in floods; President Coolidge sent his own message of warm praise. All the speakers were able men and women, eloquent and convincing, although few needed to be convinced. That easily led, sensation-loving body which is the general public joined now with her steadfast friends and came surging back to voice its belief in her. All the rancor she had incurred when she had championed the first struggling trade unions and their justified strikes, when she had stood by Governor Altgeld as he freed the unfairly condemned anarchists, when she visited Abraham Isaak who was falsely believed to have been associated with President McKinley's assassin — all that was forgotten.

William Kent, who as a very young man, had been convinced by hearing her speak and who had learned so much from his interviews with her concerning the playground, had written a letter full of his appreciation of what he had received from her. The list of those on the committee arranging for the dinner included university presidents, manufacturers, judges, lawyers, bank presidents, doctors, ministers, meatpackers, authors, editors and professors. All had had direct contact with her and her work. Mrs. Bowen was to have been toastmistress, but since she was ill Julia Lathrop presided in her place. When Jane Addams got up to reply, she said: "In a way I am humiliated by what you say, for I know myself to be a very simple person, not at all sure that I am right, most of the time not right."

It was a most memorable evening, a vindication and a triumph for Jane Addams of which she steadily declared herself undeserving. But everyone there knew what she and her associates at Hull House had stood for through those long and difficult years.

Difficult years were still to come. Not much over a twelvemonth later, she and all who were present that night faced once more a changed world. Doubts and anxiety that had been expressed but unheeded for some time suddenly changed to bitter certainty when that fateful October of 1929 saw the bubble of speculation burst. All that glittering prosperity dissolved into panic when suddenly all of those who had been planning vaguely to "get out of the market" in time, decided to do so then and there. A wave of selling on the New York Stock Exchange became an avalanche, the floor a shouting pandemonium of owners and agents offering stocks at any price obtainable. Many securities went begging with no one to take them up, securities bought earlier at fantastic prices which many purchasers could ill afford. We do not often have opportunity to measure the exact cost of unallayed panic. In this case we can. By the end of that October day's trading the losses could be reckoned as amounting to $23 billion.

Nobody, except a very few experts whose muttered words had gone unheeded, had used the word "inflation" to apply to those years when fortunes rode so high. It was so much easier and pleasanter to think that this was the natural order of things. But for the space of time which followed the stock market crash and the abrupt arrival of a new economic era, a name was very soon found — the Depression, spelled with a capital letter.

Unemployment spread as rapidly as had the influenza epidemic. Buying shrank proportionally since the vast body of working people had now no money to spend. As months went on, want grew agonizingly greater and greater. Families whose main wage-earner was laid off began to go hungry, children to show effects of malnutrition. Rents went unpaid and notices of eviction were posted on doors everywhere. Banks which could not collect their interest on mortgages began to be in trouble; one by one they closed their doors. The largest trust company in Chicago collapsed and the life savings of hundreds of depositors disappeared. There seemed no way of understanding what was taking place nor where it would lead. The poor, hardest hit of all, tried to close their ranks and help each other as they had always done. But the effort was in vain. There was simply not enough for everyone.

The Pullman Company, still keeping the founder's name although he had long been dead, had in the past years built up a reserve fund sufficient to carry on their work without discharging their employees. They had learned their lesson in that other depression called the Hard Times. But in this crisis of the early nineteen-thirties very few had possessed the foresight to do the same. Extraordinary financial practices were being uncovered everywhere, such as borrowing and lending on incredibly flimsy security. Policies that had once been admired as bold were now seen to have been foolhardy beyond belief. At all levels of society there was grievous loss.

Among the vast army of industrial employees the situation was desperate. The social workers, numerous now and practiced in observation, were united in declaring again that the state, county and city systems of relief were completely beyond their depth and totally unable to cope with the gigantic task. They were not equal to giving support to the staggering economy and meeting the needs of thousands, finally millions of destitute families. The federal government alone could possibly take the necessary measures.

Few expressions have been more unjustly applied than in the designation of this national tragedy as the "Hoover

Depression." Herbert Hoover certainly had no more to do with causing it than had any other American citizen who watched industry make its mistakes without realizing the possible results. Very few Presidents have been so confronted by crisis as he was toward the end of his administration. He had been elected on the basis of his really magnificent accomplishment in administering relief to starving Europe, a huge task, but a far simpler one than this which was before him now. Hoover was an engineer and he had certain ideas that the fault lay in geographical distribution, and could be remedied. His real genius was for organization. People who worked under him have testified that his executive machinery was a marvel of smooth-working efficiency. Neither he nor anyone else could see at once the total extent of the tragic situation. A thrifty Quaker, he hesitated to open the floodgates of spending from the national funds which seemed to be required.

By the time Franklin Roosevelt was elected in 1932, the extent of the disaster, was more fully realized. Franklin Roosevelt had a sense of people even more than of material resources. He was, moreover, a shrewd judge of the capabilities of individual persons and secured some invaluable advisers, to whose counsel he listened. He was the fourth President to take active note of the qualities of Jane Addams and to acknowledge her as a truly great humanitarian. Of these four, the first and last were Roosevelts. Teddy Roosevelt differed sharply with her concerning peace but never lost his high regard for her. Woodrow Wilson had taken over certain items of her program of reform and a Democratic administration had carried them out. Herbert Hoover made good use of her abilities in bringing public opinion to support relief and rationing programs. Franklin

Roosevelt, to whom Frances Perkins introduced Jane, was to appreciate her warmly.

Aiding Hoover in the administration of the Belgian and French relief plans, Jane had learned to be an expert on food conservation. She passed some of that knowledge to his successor. Frances Perkins tells of hearing a conversation between her and Franklin Roosevelt during a visit to the White House. Because of unemployment, restrictions on immigration were under discussion. There had been that year a bountiful harvest and a great overproduction of wheat which had so reduced prices that the farmers were in difficulties. "Those bushels of wheat," Jane said to the President in her gentle voice, "I figured it out the other day. It is just about what a million immigrants a year would have eaten up."

Eleanor Roosevelt, long interested in social work, was a warm and admiring friend. Jane speaks of being asked to a family dinner at the White House, when the President, a genial host, did the carving himself.

Frances Perkins tells of her interview with Franklin Roosevelt after his election and before he was inaugurated. She was summoned to see him at his house in New York City on East 65th Street. The place when she arrived was a scene of confused preparation for the great change in the life of the Roosevelt family. Packing was going on everywhere, visitors were crowding in and out; there was an office on the first floor jammed with reporters. But upstairs, where Franklin Roosevelt's study was, peace and quiet prevailed.

A secretary asked her to wait, which she did, in company with "a stocky blond man" who evidently also had an appointment with the President-elect. He was called in,

JANE ADDAMS

then, some time after, she was summoned. Mr. Roosevelt, sitting at his desk, introduced the blond man, Harold Ickes, the same liberal-minded lawyer whom Jane Addams had enlisted to see that justice was shown the victims of the panic that followed the death of the Jewish boy Averbuch. That morning when Frances Perkins met him, Ickes had received his Cabinet appointment as Secretary of the Interior. When he was gone, Roosevelt gave his reason for summoning Miss Perkins.

"I've been thinking things over," he declared, "and I've decided I want you to be my Secretary of Labor."

He had said earlier that he intended to have a woman in the Cabinet. To head the Department of Labor, however, would be a most difficult assignment having to do with the working man and all his needs and complaints, both justified and unjustified, and with the whole body of labor, just then divided into two warring sections — the C.I.O. (Congress of Industrial Organization) and the A.F.L. (the American Federation of Labor).

She responded at once that, while it might be appropriate enough to have a woman at the head of the department since there were so many women now in industry, it was much wiser to have a person who was a representative of the ranks of labor itself, as there had always been so far. His answer was that he and she together had accomplished much for the state of New York while she was industrial commissioner and that they could do as much for the whole United States. He was not to be moved by any of her arguments.

She said finally that if she accepted she would ask support for an ambitious program, which she outlined in concentrated terms. It called for immediate measures for the relief of those in want on account of unemployment. It would include also a study looking toward a federal law to regulate wages and hours in industry, establish old age and unemployment insurance, abolish child labor, and create a federal employment service.

Here was much the same program for which Jane Addams and Hull House stood, plans which Frances Perkins had heard discussed night after night by that extraordinary group of which she was one. She could recollect Florence Kelley with her fiery belligerence, Julia Lathrop with her quick insight and gracious diplomacy, the two young Abbott sisters, Grace and Edith, newly established as residents and full of enthusiasm and great promise. There was Mary Rozet Smith with her patient wisdom. Above all there was Jane Addams with her penetrating, sympathetic philosophy which took note of the rich as well as the poor, of the possible as well as the impossible, above all of the desires and necessities of youth.

Through the whole length of those years they had all toiled in their own places for just such reforms, developing and formulating them, often feeling themselves on the verge of victory, again and again struck down in seeming defeat when a new law was declared unconstitutional. But defeat and discouragement were never acknowledged as more than temporary. "The public must be ready for it," Jane Addams kept insisting.

The time had never seemed ripe for such a program before. But in this moment of national crisis, in the presence of an incoming President willing to risk his political reputation and ready to achieve the apparently impossible, with willing helpers who could fully understand the depth of the need and the height of the difficulties, the time was *now*.

After Franklin Roosevelt was inaugurated in March, there followed an awakening of new spirit everywhere, encouraged by the prospect of novel and courageous measures to deal with the emergencies of the Depression. But conditions could only be described as desperate. At the very moment of the inauguration ceremonies, banks were failing right and left and wild panic seemed imminent. The new President's first order was to close all banks. A landslide of failures was thus arrested, and the energetic Chief Executive went forward with drastically thorough measures.

Public opinion supported him; a sleeping public conscience had at last been frightened broad awake. It was clear what harm had been done by long indifference to the welfare of certain sections of society and to the dangerous fact of poverty. Too great attention to the sole purpose of making money had absorbed too many people.

The New Deal came step by step to full action. A floor was put under wages, to prevent their going lower than a level of decent existence. A ceiling was put upon hours so that they could not go beyond a reasonable limit, even in rush seasons. The President set up a new Federal Relief Commission to replace the organization with limited powers and resources inaugurated by Herbert Hoover. To be chairman of this commission he named Harry Hopkins, a former settlement worker, who was put to work so precipitately that there was no office available in the building his organization was to occupy. A desk had to be set up for him in the hall. The report has come down that, from this point of vantage, and in the first two hours of his incumbency he distributed five million dollars.

XIX

"Who Is My Neighbor?"

Franklin Roosevelt had impulsively acceded to the program of reform measures proposed to him by Frances Perkins. She warned him that they might frame bills for social legislation and get them passed only to see them judged later to be unconstitutional, as had happened so many times earlier. But the President did not hesitate. "We can work out something when the time comes," he insisted.

His designated Secretary of Labor made no delay in commencing to carry out this vast undertaking. By the time of Roosevelt's first Cabinet meeting, she was able to announce that she had called a conference of labor leaders to draw up a program for relief of unemployment and for a plan for public works. It would take too long to enumerate here the list of legislative measures which were passed, sometimes with ease, sometimes with great difficulty. They were emergency measures for work, for direct relief from want, for the regulation and maintenance of health and safety. All of them had the enthusiastic even if necessarily intermittent support of the President. They always had the careful attention of the Secretary of Labor.

Overall it was a bold plan for the rescue of a nearly ruined economy. Robert Wagner, Senator from New York, and Representative David Lewis played a large part in getting the program made into law. Most of the important measures were declared to be constitutional, with one vital exception. The Administration had indeed worked out a great deal. Meanwhile long and careful preparation was going forward on the so-far most important piece of legislation of all, the act for the Social Security Administration.

President Roosevelt had set up a special Cabinet Committee on Economic Security to put this act in form. Frances Perkins was chairman, and Harry Hopkins one of the members. F.D.R. took immense interest in it although he had little time to devote to any one project. In a message to Congress he had declared that a Social Security measure would provide "against the hazards and vicissitudes of life." His early idea was that security coverage should be "from the cradle to the grave," but he was dissuaded from this as being not yet practical.

Frequent consultations were held with the Children's Bureau. Julia Lathrop had retired in 1921 and Grace Abbott, also of Hull House, was now director. Lengthy hearings were being held before committees of Congress. Most items in the bill were not new. Provisions for insurance against unemployment and the needs of old age had been talked about at Toynbee Hall when Jane Addams first went there before Hull House opened. She had carried the ideas back with her to be reviewed and adjusted to a different economy and a different society. The full prohibition of child labor was considered for inclusion but was regretfully put aside. Such a step had still so many powerful enemies that to insist upon it was to invite failure of passage for the whole act. The entire work of preparation promised to cover months.

The period of those early nineteen-thirties was very hard for Jane Addams on account of the great distress which surrounded her and Hull House, against which all of them were working day and night. But the days were to bring her also moments of gratifying pleasure. The tributes of the dinner at the Furniture Mart were followed by a succession of honors heaped upon her from many directions.

She was given an honorary degree of Doctor of Laws by Yale University, the first ever offered to a woman. There was another L.L.D. from Rockford, which she had helped to make into a college. Other colleges and universities followed with similar honors, including a degree from Swarthmore College in recognition of her prominence in women's work for peace. In her will she bequeathed all of her papers and letters to their library for safekeeping, where they now remain in the college's notable Peace Collection.

The Furniture Mart dinner was matched in 1929 by the celebration of Hull House's fortieth year. Up to that time there had been six hundred residents, many of whom came to achieve great distinction. A future prime minister of Canada had been one of them. What was probably closer to Jane's heart was that many of the members of classes and clubs had made brilliant successes in music and art schools. Many a young bride had learned in the sewing and cooking classes how to take care of a family properly, and many an ignorant and bewildered immigrant woman had been taught how to prepare American foods.

There were various meetings on this anniversary occasion; there were speeches and more speeches. Dr. John Dewey, once the fiery and controversial young professor at the University of Chicago and now one of America's leading philosophers and educational leaders, was there to speak of his lifelong friendship with Hull House and its head. There were many other notable guests, all there to do honor to Jane and to rejoice with her over the success that Hull House had been for twoscore years. Later Jane would publish her account of the *Second Twenty Years at Hull House*.

She had kept insisting that people should not come to be residents there for the purpose of learning to be professional social workers. Settlements were founded to give immediate help to persons in need, and at the same time to develop and carry out long-term plans for a wider and deeper knowledge of the social evils that underlay poverty, and their possible remedies. A settlement was not a formalized institution. Its purpose was to seek out new ways and to follow them in any direction that opened, to learn facts by direct contact with friends and neighbors, with poverty itself.

The success of her fundamental approach was widely realized from 1931 onward, even when people's minds were preoccupied with the problems and discomforts of the Depression. She was one of the few bright lights in the midst of that dark time. Further honors of every kind began to rain upon her. A prominent women's magazine pronounced her to be "the first among twelve of the greatest living women of America." Later in the same year she was noted as one of the six most outstanding present-day Americans, the other five being men. Her large service to young Greeks who went home from Chicago to fight for

"Direct contact with friends and neighbors" at Hull House

their country during the war was rewarded with the Greek Republic's Medal of Military Merit. In 1931 the Alumnae of Bryn Mawr College presented her with the M. Carey Thomas prize of five thousand dollars for her great contribution to American living.

Theodore Roosevelt had pronounced her "the best argument for women's suffrage." He had been right and now everyone seemed to realize it. In December of the same year as the Bryn Mawr award, she received notice that she was to share with Dr. Butler, the president of Columbia, the Nobel Prize for services to peace. She was ill in a hospital in Baltimore at the time, and was unable to go to Sweden to receive it, so the American ambassador accepted it for her. If one more thing were needed to reestablish her in public confidence and favor, this award accomplished it.

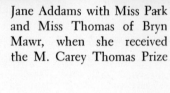

Jane Addams with Miss Park and Miss Thomas of Bryn Mawr, when she received the M. Carey Thomas Prize

Jane Addams at about the time she received the Nobel Prize

All of Dr. Alice Hamilton's available time was still spent at Hull House, for Jane Addams's health was her particular regard. Jane's illnesses were fairly frequent and there was never any knowing when another might occur. Alice Hamilton kept vigilant watch over her and was one of the very few who could persuade her to keep in any measure within the limits of her strength. Their journeys together were many.

The dedication to Jane's book *The Excellent Becomes the Permanent* reads: "To Alice Hamilton, whose wisdom and courage have never failed me when we have walked together in the very borderland between life and death." The small volume is a collection of addresses she made at the funerals of persons very near to her. They show, beyond anything else that she has written, her clear faith and her steady belief in God. The moving occasions upon which she spoke brought out to the full the tenderness and understanding of which she was so capable.

She spoke of Jenny Dow and "the piercing sorrow" of contemplating the death of a young mother with small children. She called Henry Demarest Lloyd, who worked so indefatigably for the pardon of the men condemned for the Haymarket Riot, "a valiant defender of Democracy." As she spoke of the eight-year-old son of John Dewey, she did not stress that bitter frustration a parent feels in the death of a child, knowing the future he had envisioned was not to be. She said only, "His future will exist without relation to ourselves." That very borderland of death of which she spoke in the dedication had been more than once Jane's own, at times terrifyingly near.

The progress of that program of carefully planned reform had been continuous. The Social Security Act was almost ready to submit to Congress. Earlier legislation began at last to relieve somewhat the harshness of the Depression; people were beginning to get glimpses of its real nature and of why it returned in cycles with ever-increasing severity.

A great meeting took place in Washington in April 1935, of the worldwide association of the Women's International League for Peace and Freedom, which Jane Addams had helped to found. She was the central figure. There were pictures and interviews beforehand and in the evening an immense dinner at the Willard Hotel. Mrs. Roosevelt spoke, as did Secretary Ickes and Sidney Hillman. The president of the General Electric Company offered a tribute also, labor and management thus being represented in acknowledgment of Jane's services to society. At the end she rose to reply.

"I do not know any such person as you have described here tonight," she declared.

For the next day a huge world radio hookup had been prepared. The British ambassador introduced Lord Robert Cecil speaking from London, the Japanese ambassador introduced Prince Tokugawa speaking from Tokyo. Paul Boncour spoke from Paris. There were others from all quarters, each giving tribute to Jane Addams, to her work and to her ideals for peace.

Jane might well have been exhausted by this gigantic ovation, but she returned immediately to Chicago in the best of health and spirits. She said of the Washington experience, "I liked all of it. They made me feel as though I were still in the front line trenches." In that spirit she attended on May 10 a meeting of the Cook County Commission to discuss funds for relief.

Five days later, while she was at Mrs. Bowen's house, she

was suddenly taken ill. She had been through so many illnesses, so many operations. Here was one more illness; one more operation. She had faced danger before; she faced it now without dismay. With Alice Hamilton by her side she entered that borderland again — and crossed it. She died on May 21, 1935.

Jane Addams had always been quite content with the knowledge that some of the reforms for which she worked could not be completed in her own time. She did not live to see the Social Security Act pass, the crowning effort of that long series of new and constructive measures which the Depression had brought into being. But President Roosevelt had sent a message to Congress on the subject in June of 1934, so Jane knew that it was coming. Through her close relations with those members of the Children's Bureau who had been part of the Hull House family, she had been kept informed of the ups and downs of its course through Congress. It passed finally and became law on August 14, 1935, two and a half months after Jane's death. It bore in its own way the fruit of her untiring endeavor and that of her associates. Many of its elements emanated from Hull House; many had their origin in the mind of Jane Addams herself. All of its ideas had received her steady support and the advantage of her penetrating comment.

Three years after the passage of the Social Security Act it was followed by another of almost equal importance, the Fair Labor Standards Act. Its passage occupied the full attention of the Children's Bureau, since it at last dealt boldly with the question of child labor. Grace Abbott, successor to Julia Lathrop, was no longer director; in her place was now Katherine Lenroot. She had not been a resident of Hull House, but she was often a visitor there for purposes of consultation, since Jane Addams was her warm friend and ally.

It was owing to Miss Lenroot's vigorous effort while the act was being formulated, that it included specific restrictions on the labor of young people. Those toiling children of ten, eleven and twelve years old were to be seen in industry no more. The age limits — sixteen years for certain jobs of certain hours, eighteen years for almost all of the ordinary ones — gave opportunity for decent schooling and for healthy growth. Thus ended the long war with its many grievous battles, a war of forty years' duration, that had begun at the door of the Illinois State House when Jane Addams and her small delegation came in to lay their draft of the first factory law before Governor Altgeld.

As we look back on those years of her service at Hull House, what seems to be her paramount contribution? Was it her successful effort to awaken a blind and careless public conscience to the fact of every person's responsibility to his fellow man, the duty of society as a whole to accomplish and preserve its own welfare? Was not the most telling feature of that effort the unconquerable spirit with which she came to the defense of youth?

And what, indeed, of the youth for which Jane Addams had been so concerned all her life, for whom she had planned and toiled and hoped for so long? Youth today needs a Jane Addams again. Youth will always need such a leader, for every generation emerging into adult life has to learn the hard lesson of adjustment to an unheeding world, a world which changes so rapidly that no tradition, no established precepts can bring full counsel about how that adjustment can be achieved. Not every growing generation can have a Jane Addams as its spokesman. In the absence of such a leader, society as a whole must step into the breach as Hull House did, to supply interest and understanding and good counsel.

Throughout Jane Addams's long service, the weathercock of public opinion had by turns swung south to hold her in esteem and reverence, north to cry abuse on all that she was doing. Yet in all that time she had been constant in her beliefs, unswerving in her own integrity, had always been Jane Addams, friend of youth, mistress of Hull House, a peerless neighbor, a very great lady.

Index

Abbott, Edith, 172, 201, 251

Abbott, Grace, 172, 201, 251, 261–262; director of Children's Bureau, 254

Adams, John, 5

Addams, Alice, 6, 9, 20, 35–36; marriage to Harry Haldeman, 19

Addams, Anna Haldeman, 9, 13, 15–16, 19, 33; after husband's death, 34; accompanies Jane to Europe, 36, 38, 42

Addams, Isaac, 5

Addams, Jane: early childhood, 2, 6, 8–17; and her father, 3, 8–9, 12–16, 29–30, 35; described, 8–9, 21; sense of professional mission, 9, 40–41; avid reader, 11–12; and her stepmother, 13, 15–16; first social work call, 14; pioneering spirit, 18–19; schooling, 19–24, 27–32, 35; as debater, 23–24, 160; as writer, 25, 180; gift for friendship, 26–27, 49; and religion, 28–30, 38–39, 183–184; health, 29, 35–36, 38, 40, 145, 257–259; marriage offers, 30, 38; and medical career, 34–35; travel abroad, 36–40, 145, 214, 226, 240–241; financial independence, 39, 235; and Samuel Barnett, 42–43; establishment of Hull House, 45, 48–63; her papers, 56–57, 175, 255; refuses donation from labor exploiter, 59–60; and neighborhood's domestic problems, 66, 84; and labor conditions, 69–70, 119–128; and Chicago's interest in Hull House, 71, 76; executive ability, 71; and Julia Lathrop, 80–87; and Chicago's political corruption, 87–94; public recognition, 94, 95 (*see also* honors accorded to *below*); and labor unions, 104–107; interest in young people, 120, 217–220; and Governor Altgeld, 134; vilification of, 136–137, 162–165, 168, 212, 224; and Tolstoy, 145–148; and child labor, 148–149; and juvenile crime, 151–152, 154–155; eulogizes Altgeld at his funeral, 167; speaking engagements, 171–172, 212; and Lillian Wald, 189; and Children's Bureau, 193, 198; and politics, 204–212; delivers nominating speech for Theodore Roosevelt, 207–208; dedication to peace, 209, 222–231, 244; belief in international friendship, 234; testimonial for, at Furniture Mart, 244–245, 255; and

Henry Street Settlement, New York, 171, 188–189, 192, 239
Hero Club. *See* Young Heroes Club
Hillman, Sidney, 109, 260
Hoover, Herbert, 225; and Great Depression, 247–248, 252
Hoover Commission, 225, 226, 249
Hopkins, Harry, 252, 254
Hughes, Charles Evans, 212
Hull, Charles, 45–46, 48
Hull House, 13, 32; described, 45–46; opened, 46, 48–49; day nursery, 49–52; and neighborhood need, 51, 119–120; kindergarten, 52–53; early problems, 53–54; and the street boys, 54–56; Young Heroes Club, 56, 129; Saturday night dances, 58; boarding clubs for working girls, 58–60, 119–120; evening cooking classes, 60; residents system, 61, 213; first Christmas, 61–62; financing problems, 62; first New Years' Day party, 62–63; Boys Club, 62, 89; Coffee Shop, 74–75, 147; playground, 76–78, 91–92; during Hard Times (1893), 79; and welfare assistance, 85; and political corruption, 86–94; Men's Club, 89–91; Women's Club, 92–93, 137; campaign against dirty milk, 94; incorporation, 95; and trade unions, 104–107; Working People's Social Science Club, 106, 135; growth and support of, 111; and labor legislation, 131, 135; Eight Hours Club, 135; vilification of, 136–137; and Louise Bowen, 137–138, 140–

141, 241; music school, 143; art school, 143; Butler Picture Gallery, 144; and Juvenile Court, 149–159; Detention Home, 156–157; Prince Kropotkin's stay at, 162; Theodore Roosevelt at, 168–169; and industrial inequality, 171; trained social workers from, 172; lack of religious services criticized, 183; and public baths, 184; and national Children's Bureau, 191; Labor Museum, 219; during First World War, 227; Octagon Room, 228; during influenza epidemic (1918–1919), 233; income and expenditures (1914–1929), 235; fortieth anniversary, 255–256
Hull House Associates, 95
Hull House Maps and Papers, 191
Hull House Players, 169
Hurd, Judge Harvey B., 152

Ickes, Harold, 107, 250, 260
Illinois, University of, 94, 162
Illinois Board of Charities, 81, 86
Illinois College, 24
Illinois Superior Court, 133
Illinois Supreme Court, 101, 141, 143
Immigrants, 69, 110; exploitation of, 173; and superstition, 216–220
India, 241
Industrial conditions. *See* Working conditions
Industrial schools, county, 151
Infant Care (Dr. Meigs), 196
Influenza epidemic (1918–1919), 232–233

International Congress of Women, 225
International friendship, 234
Interstate Oratorical Contest, Jacksonville, Illinois, 23–24
Ireland, 36; immigrants from, 69
Isaak, Abraham, 162–165, 245
Italy, 42

Jacksonville, Illinois, 23, 24
Jane Club, Hull House, 58–60, 119–120
Japan, 241
Johns Hopkins Medical School, 34, 38
Juvenile Court, 149–159, 170; probation system, 153–154; opposition of local officials, 155; and Detention Home, 156–157; and dependent children, 158
Juvenile Court Committee, 152

Kelley, Mrs. Florence, 111–114, 143, 172, 175, 177, 185; vocational adviser at Hull House, 114; and sweatshops of Chicago, 117, 119, 121–122, 123, 124, 148; and labor law, 130–131, 142; chief inspector for Factory Law, 131–132, 138–139, 141, 149; and socialism, 135; and Consumers' League, 149, 170–171, 173; fact-gathering, 173; and Lillian Wald, 188, 189; and Children's Bureau, 192, 193, 198, 200; and Committee on Occupational Standards, 205–206; and Frances Perkins, 251
Kelley, Ko, son of above, 185
Kenna, Hinky Dink, 87, 89
Kent, William, 75–77, 80, 179, 245

Keyser, Mary, 46, 48, 70–71
Kindergarten, Hull House, 52–53
Kropotkin, Prince Pëtr Alekseevich, 162

Labor, 96, 113; and collective bargaining, 108–109. *See also* Child Labor; Working conditions
Labor Commission, New York, 173
Labor legislation, 124–126, 130–133; criticism of, 132–133
Labor Museum, Hull House, 219, 220
Lathrop, Julia, 26–27, 80–87, 143, 172, 177, 185, 189, 191; and state Board of Charities, 81, 86–87; described, 82; and Hull House neighborhood problems, 84–85; and working conditions in Chicago, 114, 119, 124; and Hull House Plato Club, 120; and child labor law, 130; and socialism, 135; and dependent children, 151; and Juvenile Court Committee, 152, 154–158; and *Hull House Maps and Papers*, 191; and Children's Bureau, 193–195, 197, 198, 237; in demand as speaker, 198–199; and testimonial for Miss Addams, 245; and Frances Perkins, 251; resigns from Children's Bureau, 254, 262
League of Nations, 225
Lenroot, Katherine, 262
Lewis, David, 254
Lincoln, Abraham, 6–7, 18, 98, 129, 161
Lincoln, Robert, 105
Lindsay, Judge Ben, 154